DETAILS FOR LOCATING AND CATCHING FISH

by
Jerry Carlson

939093(

Details for Locating and Catching Fish

By Jerry Carlson

Photo on page 18 and graphic on page 78 were provided by Brad Veenstra. All other graphics and illustrations were done by Larry Mattocks. Cover photo and photos on pages 49, 61, and 121 were provided by Todd Amenrud. All layout work provided by Outdoor Outlines, Inc., publishers of The Outdoorsman's Weekly, Sauk Rapids, MN.

ISBN #0-9661906-0-2

PARK PRESS Waite Park, MN

First printing November of 1997.

Published By:
Jerry Carlson
Back Bay Marketing Company
1531 Pattison Rd.
St. Cloud, MN 56303
Published and printed in U.S.A.

TABLE OF CONTENTS

ABOUT THE AUTHOR

Jerry Carlson grew up on a widening of the Mississippi called Lake Pepin where he was able to spend a considerable amount of time studying the art of fishing with his grandfather, Walt Copp. After moving to St. Cloud, Minnesota he continued to expand upon his love of fishing and the outdoors and did as much "research" on the water as time would allow.

Jerry began his writing career in 1987 when he first started writing articles for The Outdoorsman's Weekly, published by Outdoor Outlines. Since that time Jerry has continued to expand his writing to include most of the major outdoor papers in the Midwest as well as nearly 40 newspapers through the syndicated column he writes as part of Fishing and Hunting Pro-Mo's.

In addition to writing, Jerry has also been involved with other media such as television and radio. He currently hosts "In the Outdoors" radio on WJON AM and WWJO FM stations located in St. Cloud. In addition to radio Jerry conducts many seminars each year including clinics for kids.

ACKNOWLEDGMENTS

It is not possible to write a book without help from many people. I would first like to thank my wife for her patience in allowing me to spend the amount of time fishing that I do and for being a great fishing partner when schedules allow her to go along. I would also like to thank the Fishing Pro-Mo's Team for sharing information so willingly. I would especially like to thank Todd and Randy Amenrud for their help with pictures and the writing process and Dick Winter for proofing.

There are many others that I have dragged along over the years that have been very patient in tolerating my need to mix fishing and business. This list includes Larry Mattocks, Jerry Hayenga, Neil Welman, Duane Osgood, Gary Augustine, Charlie Simkins, Jay Adams, Tom Brandt, and my brothers Jeff and Jay.

I also want to thank Jim Gerchy and the Outdoorsman's Weekly staff for their work in getting this book ready to print.

INTRODUCTION

Kids love to fish, but they don't learn it on their own. Someone has to show them how. Someone has to take the time to introduce them to this wonderful pastime.

Of all the activities that are available to us in this fast paced world, fishing is one of the most unique. Fishing is an activity that can be practiced over and over, yet there is never any hope of mastery. No matter how good your angling skills are, you will still experience days when the fish come out on top. But that is one of the beauties of fishing. You don't have to feel you are a failure if you have a down day. Everybody has down days. That is part of fishing.

Another unique aspect of fishing is that it can be experienced and enjoyed at any level you choose. An angler can be totally content fishing carp and suckers from river banks, or catching sunnies under a dock, or chasing bigger dreams at the tournament level. Each angler chooses his/her own level of participation. No matter what level, fishing is entertaining and enjoyable.

Fishing can also be enjoyed at any age. It can be enjoyed by a kid, by a family unit, by oneself, or in retirement. It is a life long pastime with few boundaries other than those we choose to give it.

I have been involved in countless "how to" fishing discussions over the years. In these discussions I have heard anglers talk about techniques that must be followed in order to catch fish. I have heard them outline endless rules necessary for success.

The best rule on fishing that I ever heard came from Dick Winter, a guide from Park Rapids, Minnesota. His simple yet truthful statement came during a radio interview I was doing with him several years ago. Winter's basic rule for fishing is that "there are no rules." It doesn't get much more basic than that.

Although I have come to understand the validity in Dick's statement, I do believe that there is one rule in fishing. That rule, simply put, is that you can't catch fish that you can't find. I am not saying that you can always catch fish if you do find them. I am saying that locating fish, regardless of species, is the first step to becoming a successful angler.

Location is the key to fishing success. It is the initial piece to the overall fishing puzzle that must be understood and solved in order to get on with the rest of the fishing game. Although there are no hard and fast rules in locating fish, there are some generalities that can be applied to most lakes. It is these general location principles that are the initial focus of this book. Catching the fish after you have found them is the second.

CHAPTER ONE:
COVERING THE BASICS

In comparison to the other animal species on this planet, we know very little about the underwater world of the fish. When you think about it, this is somewhat understandable because we cannot penetrate the fish environment to observe it as easily as we can the animal world above ground. Sure, we can tag and monitor larger fish, but we really can't easily follow their life's patterns. We are only able to view a short piece of their overall history, and that doesn't happen until fish are large enough to carry around bulky antennas and transmitters. Even then the transmitter tells us where they are but not what they are doing.

What about fish species that are too small for radio tracking? The poor sunfish and crappies would struggle trying to swim around with an apparatus that is larger than they are. For small fish, electronic tracking is simply not feasible.

We give fish too much credit for outsmarting us. Actually, we often outsmart ourselves. Remember, fish don't think.

However, there are some basics that we do know about fish that are important in understanding why they do some of the things they do. These basics apply to all fish species regardless of size.

First of all, fish are stupid, very stupid! They are not capable of thought. The fact that these stupid creatures are so adept at making us look foolish is an embarrassing concept. Even though it often seems like the lot of them have plotted against us, it is simply not the case. They are stupid and that is that.

Although fish may be stupid in terms of their reasoning ability, it is important to remember that they have been around for millions of years. Their longevity means that they are doing something right. Fish are survivors. They respond to their environment with the instincts that they are born with and they do this very well.

To understand this even better, it is safe to say that fish do not do things by accident. They do what they do for a reason. These reasons vary greatly with different fish species. Fish are programmed differently regarding their preferred surroundings, food, light, spawning temperature and so on. Knowing some basic facts about each fish species will greatly help you in understanding the location puzzle of the particular species you are after.

GENERALITIES

To take each fish species that is popular in the Midwest and break it down by its specific traits and preferences is not possible in a book of this size. There is simply too much information to share. However, in looking at fish as a whole, it is possible to understand some of their basic traits in location. It is possible to put together some generalities that will fit the patterns and lifestyles of many different fish species on many different lakes.

The lakes that these generalities apply to are typical, fertile lakes found in the Midwest and much of the rest of the country. In geological terms, these fertile lakes would fall into the Mesotrophic or middle aged lake category. We will not be looking at the patterns in huge bodies of water like the Great Lakes. If you are fishing a lake or body of water where the fish are primarily bottom feeders and not suspended feeders, the information shared in this book will apply to you. On the contrary, if you are fishing suspended fish, this may not be your best source of information.

To begin the process, let's review the old adage that claims 90% of the fish can be found in 10% of the water. From the experiences I have encountered while fishing, I am not sure I agree with this statement. It may be too generous. It may be more accurate to say that 95% of the fish are found in 5% of the water. Either way, the majority of the water in a lake holds very few fish. The majority of water in a lake is empty.

In examining this 90% and 10% philosophy a bit further it is important to note that the magical 10% is not like slicing a pie into ten pieces. Lakes don't slice. We cannot take and pick out a 10% slice of a lake and claim to have found the magical section that will hold all of the fish. It isn't that easy. The magical 10% is not all in one piece. It is broken up into tiny spots. Worse yet, these tiny spots are scattered all over the lake. Some of these fish holding spots are found in deep water, some in weeds, and some in shallow water. The trick is to learn how to identify these potential fish holding spots when you come across them. Another part of the trick is to identify the areas of a lake that have little fish holding capabilities and thus reduce the part of the lake you need to focus on.

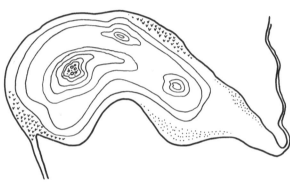

This graphic shows a typical middle aged or Mesotrophic lake. Mesotrophic lakes are the type of lakes most of us fish. These lakes have moderate to good weed growth with a variety of game fish. The game fish will be primarily bottom feeders and not suspended feeders. The older the lake the more bowl shaped they become. The younger the lake, the more structure it will contain.

This whole process isn't a very easy task. No one has ever totally figured it out so don't think you are a failure if you don't find fish every time you're at the lake. However, becoming adept at identifying and locating fish holding spots on a consistent basis can be done by anglers that choose to work at it.

Again, we are back to the concept that in order to find fish we have to recognize potential fish holding areas and eliminate areas that do not hold fish. So where do we begin? As I said earlier, we begin with some basics.

FISH ARE ANIMALS

First of all, it is critical to remember that fish are animals. They may be difficult to view and study in their underwater world, but they are still animals and relate to their environment in much the same manner that other animals do. When I am doing seminars on fish location, I tell the audience to approach fishing the same as you would approach hunting, especially deer hunting.

In order to make this hunting bit even more confusing, let's pretend for a minute that we are rabbits....yes, I said rabbits and yes, there is a correlation. Bear with me.

If we were rabbits, an animal that, like the fish, has been around for a lot of years, we would know that picking a suitable place to live is a crucial part of our overall survival. We would never pick an open field as our home for two reasons. First, there would be no food. Second, we would be easy pickings for predators. As a rabbit, life would be short in an open field.

Now think of this in terms of the fish world. Would fish be programmed to spend their days in a tenuous environment? Would they choose to live in an open area with no cover for security or food? Probably not. So why do so many anglers spend countless hours chasing fish in areas that have absolutely nothing to offer? Like rabbits and other animals, fish prefer security and to be close to food.

Nature does not allow for animal species to be careless. Nature does not give many second chances. Animal species that continually make mistakes concerning their choice of living accommodations soon become lunch and leave this planet through a process called extinction.

Let's carry this open field, rabbit scenario a little further. Let's say that instead of one rabbit in this open field, there were a hundred. Let's say that this herd of rabbits moved about as a group. Let's say they looked for food together, took turns watching for predators, and basically depended on the group as a means of protecting the individual. Now you have a situation where the survival rate of an individual rabbit has gone up. In the fishing world we call this a school.

Fish species, especially forage fish, school because that is nature's way of protecting them. It is not done by accident. Things don't happen in nature by accident. Life styles are the way they are for a reason. That reason is called survival.

In summary, it is important to remember that fish are animals. They relate to their environment much the same way that other animals do. Although they are quite stupid, they do not do things by accident. Everything they do, including traveling in schools, is done for a reason.

It is also important to note the importance of food and security. Unless the fish is at the very top of the food chain, it must be aware of living in security, yet being close to food. Fish are never far from their source of food. Find food and you will find fish nearby.

Being a successful angler by successfully locating fish is a way of thinking about what fish are logically doing. Common sense may be the most important tool we have for understanding "why" fish are where they are.

DIVERSITY

Earlier I made a statement that suggested searching for fish was much like hunting. If you have done much hunting, you have learned the value of diverse terrain. What I am referring to is hunting environments that have a variety of habitat.

Although I have not done much deer hunting in recent years, I have hunted these animals extensively in the past. Currently, I spend more time on pheasants, sharp tails, and ducks. I remember well one late season pheasant trip to South Dakota where the snow had covered up much of the cover that pheasants normally use. As we walked the fields we became quite adept at picking out specific locations within the picked corn fields that would hold birds. Anytime we found

This huge bass was caught on a rock pile located just below the weedline on a mid lake hump. Two more bass over five pounds were caught there the next day. This "spot on a spot" is a classic example of diversity.

a dip in these flat fields that contained a variety of weeds, especially thistle, there was a strong likelihood that we would flush birds.

This pattern is no different in the fish world. Fish are attracted to areas of diversity within their environment just as other animals are. Patterns for predicting these locations is simply a matter of experience and common sense. It is a matter of thinking about logical locations that would attract animals.

As we progress through this book I will continue to make reference to diversity in the fish world. **The more things you have happening in an area, the greater the likelihood you will find fish nearby.** For example, fish are attracted to cabbage beds. If that cabbage bed is located on a drop off, all the better. Add some rocks nearby, bulrushes, or coontail, and the cabbage bed becomes even more attractive. Animals like diversity and are

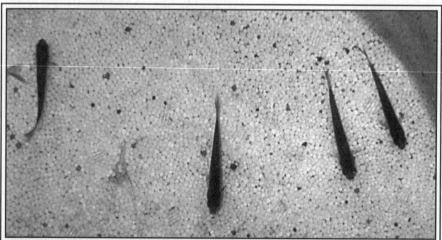

These two photos show what happens when structure is added to the environment of fish. Minnows that are scattered in the first photo cling to cover in the second.

more strongly attracted to areas that have diversity than areas that do not.

SOMETHING DIFFERENT

If you get nothing else out of this book, remember this statement: **Fish are attracted to areas in their environment that are different.** I am not totally sure why this is true; I just know it is. I will make reference to this fact over and over. Like diversity, it is something that is terribly important when it comes to eliminating places that fish aren't and locating places that fish "might" be.

I had a chance to discuss this concept with Tony Dean during a

Fish are attracted to "things" in their environment. By fishing around things you will catch fish. The more things you have happening in an area the more fish are attracted to it. Docks with multiple boats and lifts are far more appealing than a dock by itself.

radio interview I did with him at a Madison, Wisconsin Sport Show. When I asked Tony how he felt about my belief that fish are attracted to areas in their environment that are different, he agreed. However, he felt that my statement may be too complicated. He simplified it by suggesting that people need to fish around "things." When asked to clarify "things" he suggested that docks, piers, rocks, trees, points, or weedbeds would all classify as "things." Those "things" are all places that I fish.

This whole concept of fishing around areas that are different or as Dean says, "things," is really what structure fishing is all about. In the section on structure we will go into much greater detail on what to look for.

CHAPTER TWO:
UNDERSTANDING FISH

In order to really have an understanding of where to look for fish or how to catch fish, it stands to reason that we know something about fish. You certainly wouldn't buy a vehicle without first learning something about its options and features. You wouldn't buy a boat without doing the same. Sports teams don't play each other without first acquiring as much knowledge about their opponent as possible, but we are very willing to go fishing without first gathering some basic knowledge as to what fish are all about. This chapter will focus on examining some basics about fish and fish behavior so that we can better understand why fish do what they do.

THE FIVE SENSES

I was sitting in the back of the crowd at a kid's seminar that "Fishing Hall of Famer," Randy Amenrud was presenting when he started to talk about the senses of a fish and how we should be aware of these senses in our efforts to locate and catch fish. His presentation was very logical and really made me think. I have since dedicated part of my seminars to the senses.

We relate to our world through our senses. Fish do the same. Because they live in the water, their senses have different physical conditions to deal with. So although we have similar senses, how they are used and the messages they send to the brain are not the same.

Take sight for example. The eyes of a fish are not designed for viewing things at a distance. They don't need to. Water is a

We relate to our world through our senses. Fish do the same. Although we have similar senses, interpretation of senses in the water is different than our interpretation of senses in the air.(1. Feeling is done through the lateral line. Fish feel vibrations and movement in the water through water displacement, 2. Hearing is done through an internal ear, 3. Sight, 4. Smell, 5. Taste) limiting factor. No animal can see great distances under water. Water clarity and light refraction do not allow for long range visibility. So it only makes sense that if fish eyes are not made for long range vision because they can't use it, their eyes would be designed for short range vision. This is a fact. Remember, Mother Nature doesn't do things by accident.

Just how good is the short range vision of a fish? It is actually difficult to tell completely because every time we put them in an eye exam room they get excited and start flopping. Seriously, from everything scientists have been able to determine, the close range vision of a fish is excellent, maybe almost microscopic. If that is indeed the case, giving fish a long time to examine our bait offerings may explain some of the difficulty in catching them. If their short range eyesight is as good as scientists believe, we can be thankful that fish are as stupid as they are or we would never catch anything.

There is a lot of controversy as to how fish see colors. Again, it is hard to know exactly. We do know that different species of fish see some colors better than others. For example, walleyes have more green color receptors in their eyes than any other color receptor. Maybe that is why lime green and chartreuse are such good walleye colors.

Northerns, on the other hand, have more red receptors in their eyes than any other color receptor. That may explain why they love to hit fluorescent orange and why red and white dare devils have been so popular over the years.

Light is another important factor in how fish see color. Light rays are filtered out as they travel deeper into the water. This means shorter light waves, such as blue and purple, are able to penetrate deeper into the water. Other light rays do not. Colors, as we see them on the surface, are not seen the same in poorly lit water.

Still another important factor in understanding fish and how their eyes work is knowing that they cannot blink. Fish have no eyelids and their pupils do not dilate. If we had this same problem, we would be very conscious of seeking out light conditions that would be favorable for our eyes. In the fish world, this means seeking shade or going to depths where the light is filtered out. In short, **fish physically change location to find "just the right" light conditions**. They may do this several times a day.

I won't dispute the fact that there are times when large, adult fish are found very shallow and in bright sun. Spawning urges or location of food will have an effect on their location. I am not suggesting that it is impossible for fish to tolerate bright light. They just avoid it when possible. **This fact is especially true for walleyes.**

HEARING AND FEELING

I am going to lump these two senses together because they are so closely related. We seem to read so much about the lateral line of fish. This lateral line feels vibrations in the water and can sense water displacement waves such as the ones caused by another fish swimming, a lure wobbling by, or the motion of a boat overhead. Yet fish also have a sense of hearing through an actual internal ear. Through a combination of the two, fish are extremely connected to the noise level and vibration waves that are transmitted through the water.

Although sight is probably the most heavily relied upon sense for feeding, sound and vibration allow a fish to tune in on an area that bait may be traveling through. As an angler this fact is helpful because fish will move to an area where vibrations are telling them there might be food. It is also important to note that the lateral line is sensitive enough that fish can use it to feed even when they can't see.

Fish have an internal ear that is capable of picking up sound 50 to 100 feet away. Rattles in artificials like this Husky Jerk, aid fish in locating lures and aid anglers in productivity.

I am sure many of you have heard stories or read about experiments with fish that are blind or at least in an environment where they can not use their sight. As a general rule, these fish are able to feed just fine. However, fish that have grown up in an environment where the water clarity is poor and where they have not been able to depend a great deal on sight for finding fish do much better in total darkness than fish that come from very clear water where they have grown accustomed to using sight as their main sense for feeding.

How sound travels in water is another important factor in determining how fish hear. When it comes to sound, water is quite different than air. Sound travels two and a half times faster in water and is magnified seven times. Every little clink in your boat is a major CLUNK in the water. Those little rattles and ticks made by your lures are very audible to the fish.

SMELL AND TASTE

At times the addition of a scent to my bait has improved my catch. Other times fish wouldn't touch a lure once scent was added. Scent is not a cure all but I do believe it has its time and place.

Fish have a very acute sense of smell. It is estimated that sharks can smell blood from miles away. Thankfully, there aren't any sharks in the lakes that I fish, but there are plenty of other fish that make use of their sense of smell for feeding purposes. Smell is one of the reasons that live bait works so well. Smell is one of the reasons fish suck in potential food to taste it. This sounds like something people would do. It is! Without a doubt people will taste something because it smells good.

To find out more about the relationship between smell and taste do this experiment. The next time you are eating something

that is quite tasty, try plugging your nose during the eating process. You will find that you have lost most of your sense of taste when the smell is gone. How similar this is to a fish is beyond me, but it is important to note that smell is a huge factor in determining what bait fish will strike.

If you are an ice angler that fishes for panfish, you probably know the importance of fresh, scent filled bait. Sometimes the only way you can catch finicky panfish is to utilize fresh smelling bait. On some days, adding new grubs to

Fresh bait gives off more scent. The crappie shown here with Allen Safranek is the result of changing grubs frequently.

your lure every 10 to 15 minutes is the only way you can get fish to bite. Fresh grubs mean fresh scent. Fresh scent means a fresh round of bites.

This short section on senses is not designed to be all encompassing, but instead is designed to give a greater understanding of what fish are all about. Hopefully, this information will help in the upcoming discussion on location.

CHAPTER THREE:
THE IMPORTANCE OF WEEDS

Not all lakes are blessed with a good weed growth, but for the lakes that are I believe that it is impossible to over emphasize the importance of weeds, especially when we are talking about locating fish. Weeds are a critical factor in the overall life cycle of fish that are found in lakes where weeds are prevalent. Weeds are important for fish in a variety of ways. The five most important attributes of weeds are food, concealment, security, shade, and oxygen.

THE FOOD CHAIN

My teaching background reveals itself when I start talking about the food found in weeds. In order to fully understand the importance of weeds as a food source we need to start at the beginning of the food chain.

The basis of all life in the water starts at the microscopic level with tiny animals called zoo plankton and tiny plants called algae or phyto-plankton. It is these microscopic critters that provide the forage base for larger animals. These so called larger animals are not all that large. Fish that are newly hatched, called fry, will feed heavily on these plankton critters. Some minnows may feed on them for most of their life. More impor-

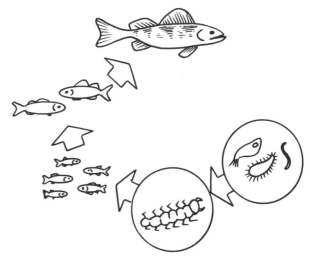

Predator fish comfortably eat forage 1/3 the length of their bodies. However, without plankton and insect larvae at the bottom of the food chain, there would be no forage fish or predators for that matter. The food chain starts at the microscopic level with zooplankton and phytoplankton.

tantly, it is the insect larvae that really chow down on this minia-ture forage base. Although plankton is the base of the food chain, it is the insect larvae that play such an important role in the life of the everyday angler.

It is estimated that for every person in the world, there are at least two million insects. It may be as high as 200 million insects for each person. Anyway you look at it, that is a lot of bugs! There are actually more than a million species of insects. That is far more than all of the other plant and animal species put together. And where do many of these insect species live? In the water.

In order to truly appreciate the quantity of bugs that live in the water, you really should have a chance to experience a hatch sometime. My most memorable experience with bugs happened to me on a trip to Mille Lacs Lake, a huge body of water located in Central Min-nesota. I had been fishing this walleye factory on a regular basis this particular summer with very good suc-cess. On this trip I happened to be guiding so I really needed to catch fish.

It never fails, just when you feel you have the pattern on

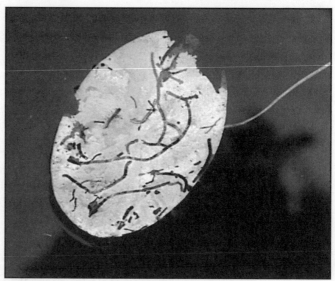

Insects are a critical part of the food chain for fish.

a lake really figured out, you get thrown a curve. As luck would have it, the curve that hit us was a bug hatch. I don't know what kind of insects these tiny little critters were; I just know that they were everywhere. They were under your glasses, in your ears, up your nose, and down your shirt. It was difficult to breathe at times because of the quantity of bugs around. Drinking coffee or eating a sandwich was impossible. Eating bugs was easy.

As expected, fishing was horrible. The hatch was a feeding

bonanza for the fish. After suffering for several hours I noticed the bottom of my green Alumacraft was starting to turn gray from bugs. Finally, one of my clients, Doug Munneke, with his shirt up over his head and the pole laying in the bottom of the boat, broke a long silence with a, "Can we go home now, please?" And we did.

To better understand this insect and plant interaction take a close look at an aquatic plant sometime. You will notice that it is full of holes, grooves, and other evidence that insect life flourishes on it. The fact that insects live in and around plant life is no secret in the fish world. Remember, fish have been around for millions of years and they know plants mean food.

ICE-OUT PANFISH AND INSECTS

I sincerely believe anglers have no idea how important insects are as a food source for many species of fish. This is always evident to me when I hear people talk about the annual spring migration panfish make to shallow water. I hear over and over about the spawning fish anglers are catching. This ice-out migration to the shallows has nothing to do with spawning. Crappies don't spawn until water temps reach the mid sixties and sunnies like it warmer still.

This early season shallow water migration is strictly a food run. Panfish, including crappies, are heading to the shallows to eat insect larvae. Crappies are not chasing minnows as many think. Yes, you can catch crappies on minnows, but it is not their major source

Many different types of insect nymphs and larvae live in the mud. Early season panfish migrate to these mud bottomed areas to take advantage of the feeding opportunities found there.

of food. I have never talked to an angler that has caught early season crappies with their stomachs stuffed with minnows. If you find a minnow in the stomach of an early season crappie it will have a hook scar on it. Somebody missed that fish! (Probably your fishing buddy.)

Think about the type of area these early season panfish are caught in. It is a shallow, dark bottomed bay, with bottom consistency that is made up of thick, oozy mud. It is true that mud absorbs the sun's energy faster than light colored areas, but just as important is what is found in the mud.

Mud is home for insect larvae. It is the winter resting place for hundreds

St. Cloud angler, Duane Osgood, is an expert at locating and catching early season crappies. He knows the importance of following the warm water and working areas of active insect larvae.

of types of insects. If you look at these quiet bay areas in the summer months you will find that they are full of weeds. They will usually be so weed choked that you would never consider looking for fish there in the summer. You can also be sure these areas are teeming with insect life. In the fall, weeds die out and sink to the bottom. So do the insect larvae.

Insect larvae become active in the warmer water of spring. The fish simply are looking for the warmest water which in turn will harbor the most active insects. If you find active insect larvae you will find fish. As a general rule I have found that the bay areas will be several degrees warmer than the main lake. In fact, I have seen bays that were ten degrees warmer than the main part of the lake.

One other important note on this early pattern is bird watching. One spring I was doing a television show with Tom Brandt from "Outdoors Minnesota." Unfortunately, we were having a difficult time finding active crappies. Finally, we noticed some swallows working an area of water in a nearby bay. Swallows eat bugs. If there was food for the birds above the water it only made sense that there would be food for the animals below the surface as well. After all, both the birds and the fish were after the same food source.

As it turned out, the fish were there taking advantage of the feeding opportunity that was present and yes, we caught fish. I have used this swallow routine over and over throughout the years. The birds are following the hatch just like the fish.

CONCEALMENT AND SECURITY

As adults we are very concerned with safety. We lock our houses at night, lock our cars when we leave them, travel at safe hours, and so on. We do a variety of things to achieve a level of security that we are comfortable with.

Fish are no different. Their two primary sources of safety are weeds and water depth. It is very important to realize that weeds are not repulsive to fish. They are at home in the weeds just like a squirrel is at home in the trees and a deer is at home in wooded areas. Fish eat, rest, and hide in weeds when weeds are present.

The interesting aspect of weeds is that the areas some fish seek out for shelter and security are the same areas others are waiting in to suck down lunch. Baitfish are found in abundance in the weeds but so are the predators that will turn them into dinner.

The life expectancy for fish no matter where they live is not very good. Small fish in particular are swimming the gauntlet every time they travel in search of food. It is estimated that more than 90% of a year's newly spawned fish never make to their first birthday. Only about 1% make it to three years. If you believe in reincarnation, don't come back as a fish!

PREDATOR FISH AND WEEDS

There are no secrets in the fish world. Predator fish know just where the food is. They are very conscious of the opportunities that are available to them in the weeds. Other than spawning, food is **the** driving force in the life of a fish. Fish are **never** far from their source of food. Eating is what their life is all about. **Understanding the predator prey relationships in the water you are fishing is a critical step in predicting where predator fish will be located.**

Because weeds are such an important source of food for baitfish, it is only logical that we need to be conscious of the importance of weeds as a potential attraction for the fish we want to catch. In lakes that have a good weed growth you will find all species of fish in and around the weeds at various times throughout the year. Many fish will relate to weed growth for most of the summer months. This is simply a matter of predators staying close to their source of food.

In the past, I have been quite fortunate to have had divers attend some of my seminars. Afterwards they visited with me regarding what they have witnessed in the underwater world of weeds. They said that fish were usually quite frightened of them and would bury themselves into the thickest weeds available. However, they also talked about frequently seeing predator fish laying in a thick clump of weeds and looking outward or towards some type of opening. These predator fish, bass, walleyes and northerns, positioned themselves to take advantage of the weeds for their own safety but also used the weeds as concealment for potential ambush opportunities.

Openings and pockets in weeds then become places that we should be focusing some of our fishing efforts on. Opportunistic fish are watching these openings, waiting for something to come along that is too good to pass up. These openings are the structure or "different" areas that fish are attracted to.

SHADE

Earlier, in a section on senses, I talked about some characteristics of fish eyes. If you remember, fish do not have eyelids, nor can they adjust the pupils of their eyes to different amounts of light. This means that if their eyes are uncomfortable with the conditions they are in, they must seek out different conditions. The eyes cannot adjust so the fish does.

This is no small factor in the lives of fish. From my experience, it is only the tiny fish that don't ever seem to be bothered by light. Predator fish, the ones we want to catch, are rarely found in brightly lit water. The exception to this would be bass. Big bass will spend time in well lit environments.

I am not sure why small and young fish seem to be bothered less by light than larger fish. My guess is that they are bothered just as much as the adult fish, but they are forced into the shallows to avoid being eaten. Maybe a little discomfort from the brightness of the light is better than the darkness of a stomach. Then again, maybe fish are like children and have not gained the maturity to be concerned with items like discomfort. The point is the same. **Predator fish seek out areas that they want to be with the most dominant predator fish controlling the best areas. Smaller fish take what is left over.**

Weeds do more than filter sunlight by creating shade. The weeds also filter out the warming effects of the sun which causes heavily weeded areas to be cooler than other more open areas. Because fish are cold blooded creatures, they are comfortable in any temperature of water. However, different species of fish prefer certain temperatures which they readily seek out. Shaded weed areas can provide just the right mix of light and temperature for many different species of fish.

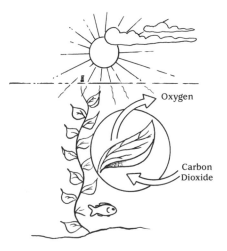

Plants play an important role in keeping water oxygenated. Through photosynthesis they remove carbon dioxide from water and put back oxygen.

OXYGEN

Oxygen is one other important benefit that weeds bring to a lake. In nature's scheme of things it is important to note that there must be some sort of system for replenishing material that is consumed. The general population of people has never figured this out, but Mother Nature does her best under the circumstances.

One element that is consumed on a daily basis by all animals both in and out of the water is oxygen. Plants are the factories that keep replenishing this supply. Not only do they replenish the oxygen, they also remove the gas that is a waste product of animals, carbon dioxide. This recharging of the oxygen supply in the water is very critical to the survival of fish, especially in winter.

It is often thought that plants are not active in the winter, but many are. In the natural cycle of plants, some die in the fall of the year and begin growth again in spring. As these plants die off the decay process that consumes them takes oxygen out of the water. To have some plants that are green and active year round is good for a lake.

I had someone ask me at a seminar about the oxygen factor and just how important it was to location. In most situations, oxygen is dispersed quite rapidly so I am not sure how many fish are in the weeds simply because they like the higher content of oxygen found there.

SUMMARY

To understand that fish relate to weeds, especially in open water conditions, does not take a genius. Weeds are extremely important in the whole scheme of fish location. Fish have everything they could ever need found in the weeds. If you have weeds in the lakes you fish you will find that fishing in and around weeds will make you successful a greater share of the time.

CHAPTER FOUR:
LOCATING FISH IN WEEDS

SO MANY WEEDS....SO LITTLE TIME

In a typical lake where anglers are chasing bottom feeding fish, there is an absolute abundance of weeds for fish to be in. The problem the angler faces is where to begin? With so many weeds, it is nearly impossible to fish them all. A half hazard approach may put you on fish but it also can be terribly time consuming. If it takes too much time to find fish, we tend to lose interest. We don't want that to happen!

There are several specific areas in weeds that tend to hold fish. If nothing else, identifying these areas will at least tell you where fish aren't. This is important because it helps reduce the 90% of the water that fish seldom use. It also helps establish patterns that are not working. That too is important. **If what you are**

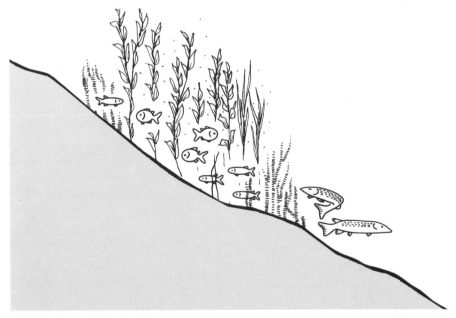

Diversity comes in many forms. Weeds, rocks, humps, points, and docks are all examples of diversity. The more diversity you find in one place, the better chance you have of finding fish there.

doing is not working, change it! Plain and simple.

One factor I frequently look for when analyzing the potential of weed beds is diversity. Diversity happens when there are several different plant types growing close together. Think of what diversity in plant growth looks like above the ground where it is easy to recognize. We can quickly see that a combination of tall, medium, and short growing plants creates a habitat that is attractive to many different animal species. It is the same in the water. Show me a place with good vegetation diversity and I'll show you a place where fish can be caught.

Diversity exists in more than just vegetation. Diversity also comes in other non vegetation forms. Examples of this would be rocks, drop-offs, docks, points, open pockets, and humps. You maybe recognize these items as the "things" that Tony Dean was referring to in chapter one. In case you haven't noticed yet, these "things" we keep referring to are items we normally call structure.

When I first moved to Central Minnesota I spent the majority of my fishing time throwing Johnson Silver Minnows tipped with pork frogs into lily pads in search of bass. After doing this on a consistent basis for several years I learned a real lesson about diversity. Lily pad beds are not all created equal.

Some pads always seemed to hold fish while others rarely did. One factor that determined the productivity of a pad bed was the

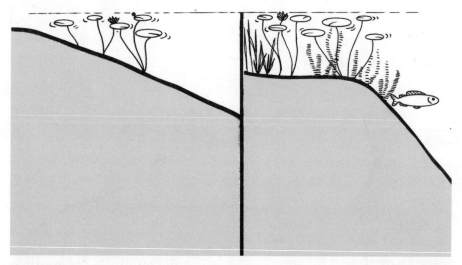

Lily pads that have weed growth mixed in with the pads are much more apt to hold bass and panfish than lilies that are clean underneath. Add deep water nearby and the pads get better still.

diversity of the weeds that grew in and around the pads. If the pads were fairly clean underneath, they were pretty worthless for holding bass.

On the flip side of this, if the pads had coontail, or northern milfoil growing in it fish were more likely to use it for feeding. I also noticed that beds with good weeds would often attract fish all day long. Beds with poor diversity in weed growth were strictly an early morning and late evening proposition.

The very best beds of all were the ones that not only had good weed diversity mixed in with the pads but were also in close proximity to deep water. Deep water also greatly improved the potential of lily pad beds with poor weed growth. Deep water allowed bass to move in to feed yet travel very little distance from the security of the depths. Diversity in the type of weeds available is important but so is diversity in other non weed related areas as well.

With experience, we became very adept at picking out lily pad beds that were going to hold fish as well as the areas within these beds that had the most potential. A visual observation of the area quickly eliminated much of the unproductive water that was not worth fishing.

It is easy to recognize diversity in water where you can visually see the bottom. Through your own experiences you will soon learn the do's and don'ts of fishing these areas. But what about places where you can't see the bottom which is going to be the situation in most of the lake? This is where your electronics come into play.

EYES TO THE BOTTOM

It may seem a bit odd to throw in a section on electronics in the middle of a discussion on weeds and diversity, but actually, it fits very nicely here. It doesn't do much good to explain the type of situations that attract fish if you have no means of locating those environments. Your electronics are your **eyes to the bottom**. They are your means of identifying the parts of a lake you can't see.

This is critical! Some type of depth finder is extremely important to overall fishing success for most anglers. I say most because there is an exception to every rule.

One of the best anglers I ever knew was a man from St. Cloud,

If you fish from a boat you should be using some type of electronics. I have found that a Vexilar is an important tool for both my summer and winter fishing.

Minnesota named Hummer Schramm. He did not believe that modern day equipment was fair to the fish. He insisted that it was a contest between himself and the fish. Hummer was one of the most successful anglers around because he was keen at figuring out patterns. He also had a knack of being able to get back to the same location on a lake without the aid of electronics.

Frankly, I am not that good. I depend greatly on my electronics to help me understand what is happening under my boat. I depend on electronics to eliminate unproductive water and identify potentially good water. It is not necessary to spend a fortune for such equipment. There are basic units available for a reasonable amount of money. The unit I depend on greatly for both summer and winter fishing is a flasher called the Vexilar. It tells me what is happening in three colors which makes interpretation easier.

If you are not very familiar with a depthfinder and are concerned about using one, don't worry. In a short time your inability to interpret signals that you are receiving will be overcome through experience.

GOOD WEEDS AND BAD WEEDS

It won't take you very long to realize that there are some weeds that fish like and some weeds they don't like. Good weeds and bad weeds, so to speak. If there was only one weed I was allowed to fish, my first choice would be cabbage. If you do not know what cabbage looks like, you need to learn! **This broadleafed weed is literally a fish magnet for nearly all species of fish!**

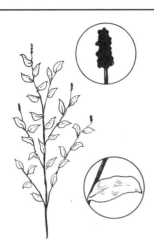

Clasping leaf pondweed, or cabbage as we have come to call it, is a fish magnet. At various times of the year you will find nearly all species of fish in a lake hanging around cabbage beds. If you find patches of cabbage, fish them!

I cannot begin to tell you the number of times I have caught fish in and around cabbage. In discussions with other anglers, I have found that they have had similar experiences. I believe there are several reasons for this.

Cabbage is a weed that is capable of growing in very deep water. (Remember, deep water is security for predators.) As cabbage grows towards the surface of a lake it tends to lose its lower leaves. This gives cabbage beds a canopy effect similar to the canopy we encounter when we walk though a hardwoods forest area. It is thick on top but more open underneath. This is ideal for fish.

Cabbage is a weed that grows all year. Sure, it dies back some in the fall and winter as well as during hot spells in the summer, but it is always green and active compared to other aquatic vegetation. Cabbage plants also harbor a vast amount of insects. This in turn brings in baitfish.

There is a small lake by my hometown, St. Cloud, Minnesota, that has good cabbage growth. Over the years I have taken walleyes, bass, northerns, crappies, and bluegills out of these cabbage beds. Some days it is hard to tell exactly what species you

These two bass, displayed by my brother, Jeff, came from a healthy clump of cabbage. They were caught on Texas rigged Culprit worms. What is not shown is the other 20 fish that came from the same spot.

will find in these beds. Rarely will we fish these beds without catching several species. Sometimes one species, such as crappies or bass will be the most prevalent. By traveling to another stand of cabbage a short distance away you are apt to find different fish.

In the late 1980's I discovered a small bed of cabbage on a lake that I frequently fished for bass. Every time I worked that cabbage area that summer, I caught at least one four pound fish. It was not a big area and there were usually just a few fish in it, but they were always big. This was clearly a matter of the most dominant predators controlling the best feeding and safety conditions found in that part of the lake.

I remember a few situations where we discovered very large flats that were covered with cabbage. These areas were extremely difficult to fish. Maybe it would be more proper to say that it was very difficult to catch fish out of these areas. Although cabbage is a great fish attractant, if you have acres of it, where do you begin? You need to begin by looking for areas within the cabbage bed that are different from the surroundings. Look for areas with diversity.

Instead of just fishing, fish the pockets, fish the cabbage points, fish the outside and inside edge of the cabbage. Look at the cabbage bed as a lake in itself and find the structure within the bed that may hold fish.

One of my fishing buddies, Jerry Hayenga, and his son were on a trip to Canada. While most of the group was off chasing walleyes they decided to try their luck at locating big northerns. To make a long story short, they spent considerable time on this rocky, boulder-strewn lake with little success. Finally, they came across a bay that contained a small but distinct patch of cabbage. Their first trip through the cabbage told them that this was the area that held the big fish. Over the next several days they caught big northerns nearly every time they worked this cabbage patch.

When it comes to finding good weeds, learn to recognize cabbage and fish it no matter what lake you are on!

Coontail and northern milfoil are two more weeds that I have good success fishing around. Both of these weeds are similar in structure. They both look somewhat like a Christmas tree as they grow into long squirrel tail looking branches. They can be found in fairly good depths and do attract fish.

One other unique fact about all three of these plants is that they are hardy. They tend to green up quickly in the spring and stay green very late into the fall, especially coontail.

It is extremely difficult to describe weeds that are bad weeds or commonly called "junk weeds" because there are dozens of different types. As a general rule these weeds are soft and flimsy and are hard to fish because they break off easily and stick to your lure. Although these weeds do hold fish they usually do not hold the quantity of fish that better weeds do.

Northern milfoil (top) and coontail (bottom) are two excellent aquatic plants for attracting fish. Next to cabbage, coontail is my favorite weed to fish.

The most important fact to remember about good and bad weeds is that each lake is different. Each year is different. Fish will relate to weeds according to the type of weeds present, forage location, cover, diversity, and season of the year. It is certainly possible to have fish ignore a specific weed on one lake and thrive in it on another. Other factors, like forage base, do help determine how good or bad a weed type

The exotic plant, Eurasian milfoil, is not to be confused with northern milfoil. Eurasian milfoil has more leaflets than northern milfoil and is far more prolific. Please take extra precautions to prevent the spread of this plant!

is on each individual lake.

BULRUSHES AND CATTAILS

It is impossible to talk about weeds without bringing bulrushes and cattails into the picture. Let's begin by examining bulrushes, more commonly known as reeds.

Reeds, for the most part, are a shallow growing weed but will occasionally grow from water depths of six feet. Reeds are very important in the overall scheme of nature and actually have many uses that extend far beyond their fish attracting ability. One well known fact about bulrush reeds is their ability to attract spawning fish. Examples of fish that use the reedbeds as spawning grounds are crappies, sunfish, and bass.

In the spring of the year as these reedbeds are growing up they become the target of pre-spawn and spawning fish, primarily ones that belong to the sunfish family. It is the hard bottom found in the reeds that is part of the attraction. Reeds tend to grow in areas that have a hard bottom versus a muddy, silty bottom. It is this hard bottom that members of the sunfish family like for building their nests.

Often times, pre-spawn fish will set up shop in deep water just off of the reeds. During the morning and evening they will make feeding movements up along the face of these reedbeds with the males going into the beds to check out possible spawning sites. At this time of the year fish along the reed banks are very easy to catch provided you don't get too close with your boat. Shallow fish spook easily.

Later in the year, reedbeds tend to be less productive, at least the shallow water ones that were used for spawning. Bass, in particular, will continue to use reeds as a major feeding ground provided the conditions are right. One area that has continually worked for me is to fish the edge of reedbeds that are directly adjacent to a steep drop-off. I have also found that the thicker reed bed patches are better producers than the sparse ones.

There are other unique features to consider when fishing reeds. One fact that I have noticed is all species of fish are usually located towards the edges of the beds. They are rarely in the middle. This fact is not true if you have open water channels in the reedbeds. These channels are roadways that fish will readily travel and should be fished.

It is not uncommon to actually see the fish you are trying to catch when fishing bulrush reeds. With a good pair of polarized sunglasses it is very likely that you can make visual contact with the fish and cast accordingly. This is especially true of spawning fish. Again, most of the fish you will see in reeds are bass, sunfish, and crappies.

One other area of reedbeds that you don't want to leave out is the very inside edge. This shallow edge doesn't seem like it would be any good, but it can be dynamite!

Think of reedbeds as a whole structure area in itself. Look at it as points, islands, inside curves, and so on. Approach the problem of solving reedbed fish by looking at the whole picture. By doing so you can pretty well predict the places that fish are going to be.

CATTAILS

Cattails are another matter. Their thickness often limits how far a fish can penetrate them. With reeds, fish are able to swim around and cruise for food. In a good stand of cats, the pure thickness of

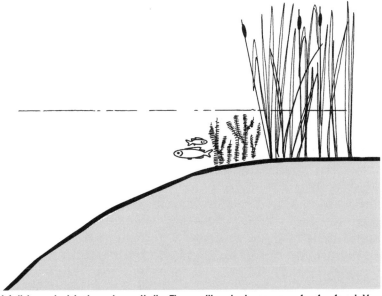

Summer and fall bass hold close to cattails. They will not chase very far for food. You may need to almost hit them on the head with your lures. Weedless lures such as spinnerbaits and plastic worms work well.

the weed often makes swimming anywhere but on the edge impossible. The edge then, becomes a key.

If you take a close look at the face of a cattail stand you will find that it is quite complex. It will be loaded with small points and pockets that have fish holding potential. Cattails are have even more potential if the front face is adjacent to fairly deep water. Deep water just adds security for the fish that are using it.

Although the front face of cattails is primarily a bass location, it can also be ideal for crappies, sunfish, and northerns, depending on the time of the year. Bass found on the front face of cattails will hold **extremely** tight. Accurate casting is absolutely critical.

Some cattails do not grow in thick stands but tend to be more spread out. These cats will also hold fish. They are probably more appealing to a wider variety of fish than thick cattails although I have found them to be less productive. Loosely clumped cattails should be fished from all angles if possible. You can never be sure just which side the predator has picked for the ambush site. All too often we tend to ignore the inside edge of emergent weeds.

Both bulrushes and cattails hold potential for yielding fish. As a general rule, these areas will be more productive early in the year and late in the year. If you are not finding the fish that you expected in these areas, move on to more productive locations.

WEEDS AND THE SEASONS

Like everything else in lakes, weeds go through seasonal changes. These seasonal changes have a great deal to do with when and where fish are found in the weeds. Let's start with the spring of the year.

If there is one time of the year good weed growth is critical for holding fish, it is probably spring. When you think about it, this is the time of year there are the fewest weeds of all because they have not had time to grow. Because of this, fish are forced to be more concentrated in areas where there is ample growth. This concentration of fish applies to both predators and prey.

It starts with the prey. Because there is so little cover available for them, they take advantage of what the lake has to offer. Predators, in turn, seek out weeds because of the forage base that is found there as well as the opportunity for ambush.

In an interview I did with Dave Csanda, editor of <u>In-Fisherman</u> magazine, he described the early season weedbeds as "remnants of last year's weeds with some new growth mixed in." He also described them as "underutilized fishing spots, especially for post spawn walleyes." He went on to explain that walleyes will often spend considerable time in these weedbed areas in spring especially if the weedbeds are close to spawning areas. This is because food fish, such as perch, are also relating to these old weedbeds. It sort of goes back to the adage that if you find the food you will find the fish.

Curlyleaf pondweed looks similar to cabbage but does not branch out as much and has very kinky leaves. It tends to grow early and die out in July. Fish are attracted to it when it is green and growing.

Many lakes in the Midwest have an exotic weed called curlyleaf pondweed. It is a tall stringy weed that looks somewhat like cabbage. This weed will grow in fairly deep water and is one of the first weeds to thrive after ice out. Because of this, northerns, bass, and walleyes will make use of this weed for lounging as well as feeding. I have found that well placed live bait on a sliding bobber rig fished in and around curlyleaf pondweed can be deadly during this time period.

The reason a sliding bobber works so well is the thickness of the weeds. It is very difficult to fish in the middle of these curly leaf pondweed areas, but a sliding bobber and live bait combo fished around the edges, especially the deep edge, can be very effective. Fishing a live bait rig in the middle of weeds such as this can be very frustrating.

This weed pattern is an example of how fish adapt to the conditions that are present in each body of water. It is also an example of how patterns change. This weed may be one of the first to grow in the spring, but it is also one of the first to die in summer. Usually, curlyleaf pondweed is cluttering the lake surface in early

July. It forms long stringy mats that are cursed by anglers and skiers alike. Sooner or later a wind will push the smelly, decaying plants onto someone's beach and the life cycle is complete for another year.

EARLY SEASON CABBAGE

Earlier, I mentioned the importance of cabbage as an area for attracting fish. Like curlyleaf pondweed, it grows early. Although it does not green up instantly with ice off, it does respond quite quickly. An impressive fact about cabbage is that it will attract fish even when it is dead.

Ted Papermaster and his grandsons, Seth and David, show off some nice early season northerns taken from the edges of curlyleaf pondweed.

I remember one spring when we were chasing walleyes on a relatively shallow lake in Central Minnesota. My fishing partner for the day was Mike Howard from Fishing Pro-Mo's. Mike was very familiar with this lake and knew where the cabbage beds were located. His technique was very basic. We would simply drift, cast, or troll 1/16 ounce jigs tipped with fathead minnows through every patch of cabbage we could find. All of our fishing was done in water under seven feet deep.

Most of the cabbage was brown and dead, but it certainly didn't matter to the walleyes. In fact, other anglers that were fishing deeper were drawing blanks. The walleyes had sought out areas of food and cover which happened to be cabbage. This is exactly the scenario Dave Csanda was describing in an earlier reference to early season weeds.

Fish of many different species take advantage of weed growth that is present in the spring of the year. As the weed growth establishes itself and the weather turns to summer, fish and forage will make use of the best conditions for food and cover they have available. The difference is that during this season of plenty there are far more areas that can potentially hold fish. Even so, this summer weed pattern is my favorite time to fish.

FALL

Just as spring is a period of sparse vegetation and concentrated fish, fall can be much the same. What happens in fall is the opposite of what takes place in spring. Instead of weeds growing and multiplying, they are succumbing to the fading light and cooler water as they approach the end of their growing season. Under the right conditions, this can be a dynamite time for bass and northerns.

Some lakes that have just the right mixture of cabbage and coontail in shallow water can be an absolute fishing bonanza. In the Midwest this usually starts in late August or early September and runs up to turnover.

Much of the junk weed that grows in shallow water dies in late August. Therefore, preyed upon fish that were scattered over large flats will now be forced to find their refuge in the patches of still green weeds. These patches can be quite spread out and are usually easy to see. Predators, namely northerns and bass, will congregate around these same patches of green weeds that forage fish are using for cover.

By throwing spinnerbaits and crankbaits around these clumps you will quickly and easily find the active fish that are looking for an easy meal. Murky water is one other factor that occasionally comes into play. Frequently, lakes that have these shallow, weedy food flats are the same ones that develop murky water as the weeds start to die off. Poor water clarity will greatly work to the advantage of the angler. Fish are nervous in shallow water and will stay put much better if clarity is poor.

As far as spinnerbaits for this fall pattern, either tandem spins or single spins will work. However, I have found that tandem blades with one being a willow leaf, will allow you to fish slower and shallower than single spins. In this weed clump pattern, tandem spinners with one willow leaf seem to give off the right vibration and will usually generate more strikes than other types of blades.

If you like action and don't mind catching bass and northerns, this fall weed bite is one of the most exciting fishing opportunities of the whole year. Unfortunately, it coincides with a time most anglers are preparing to wind down the fishing season and put their boats into storage. Fall is a time when many anglers hang up their rods and start cleaning their guns.

CHAPTER FIVE:
EDGES ARE CRITICAL

To say that edges are critical areas for locating fish is probably an understatement. I don't think it is possible to emphasize strongly enough the importance of edges in the fishing world. In order to make this easier to understand, let's go back to the "fish are animals" theory I alluded to in the first chapter.

We are not very familiar with the happenings in the underwater world compared to events that take place in the animal world above ground. It is simply a matter of observance. We cannot see what fish are doing on a daily basis.

Not only can we see animals above the ground, but we can observe their tracks, droppings, trails, feathers, roosts, nests, or a host of other items that help us identify just where animals have been and what they were doing. We can't do this with fish.

Hunters would not consider hunting in an area that is void of sign. Actually, animal sign is one of the main reasons they hunt where they do. On the angling side of this issue, people will fish all day in an area that has no fish, but they have no way of knowing this. Fish don't leave tracks, make any noise, or give us many clues as to their whereabouts. This is where edges come in.

When observing animals above the ground, think about how many times you have seen them make use of edges. Edges are the roadways of the animal world. It is where they travel. It is where they congregate. It is where they feel secure.

Remember, fish are animals. They do animal things because they are part of nature. They have the same survival instincts that other animals do. They react to their underwater world the same as animals above the ground.

Think of the number of times you have seen deer, fox, turkeys, or pheasants along the edge of something. If you are a hunter, think of the number of times you have found trails that follow the edge of a swamp, the edge of a hill, the edge of a clearing, or the edge where two different types of vegetation meet. **Animals of all types utilize edges as part of their daily routine.**

A CLOSER LOOK

It would be quite a chapter if we talked about every single edge that occurred in the underwater world of fish. Obviously, we aren't going to do that. We are going to start with the edges that are the most noticeable; the surface of the water and the bottom of the lake.

It is very easy to forget about these two edges. Maybe they are too obvious. When it comes right down to it, these two edges are totally limiting to fish. They can't get any higher than the surface and no lower than the bottom. It is this limiting factor that makes these two edges so important in the life of a fish.

If you have ever been at a sport show where they have one of the big portable fish tanks you maybe had a chance to look up at the surface of the water as a lure hits. This contact may not have much of an effect from the top, but from underneath it makes a major commotion that gets the attention of all the fish. From this one simple observation you can learn a good lesson about how a small splash on the surface is a major event when you are under the water. Fish in shallow water are very conscious of what is happening on the surface. In addition, predators use the surface of the water to trap their prey. The surface is an important edge.

The same is true for the bottom of the lake. Fish are again very conscious of feeding opportunities that await them at this location. When they are close to bottom they see disturbances that are caused by the crayfish, bottom feeding minnows, insect larvae, and the like. They know how important the bottom is in their daily routine.

On many lakes you will find bottom areas that are quite soft and mucky. In situations like this you may be better off **not** trying to use the bottom as a fish attracting technique. It is possible to have such soft, oozy muck that lures or sinkers dragged on the bottom will create a huge disturbance that will actually spook fish instead of attract them.

When fishing muck bottom there are some tricks that will help. One thing you can do is to use a bit heavier weight that allows you better feel for the bottom. Once bottom is felt, lift the weight off of the bottom a short distance to keep from dragging in the mud. This will eliminate the cloud of silt that can spook fish. Another strategy is to use a long leader with a floater. The floater will get your bait up out of the mud and will also put distance between the sinker and bait.

EDGES AND WEEDS

Weeds create a whole host of important edges for fish. These edges are taking place wherever you have two different types of weeds that meet. This is especially true of weeds that are of different size or density.

Let's talk about lily pads as an example. Because lily pads grow to the surface it becomes very easy to see just where there is a distinct edge simply by observation. It is not very difficult to fish this edge because of the visual contact you have. It is also very easy to relate to the strikes you have on this edge because you can see where you are fishing. It won't take much trial and error before you realize the importance of working this edge in relationship to catching fish.

Now, put this edge under the water where you can't see it. Suddenly, the task of fishing it becomes much more difficult. I didn't say it becomes less productive or impossible, just more difficult. Once we lose the visual contact with edges, it is easy to stray onto something else. **This is absolutely, positively the wrong thing to do.**

Here again we fall back to why fishing is difficult. Knowing where fish are that you can't see is not easy. Knowing the type of

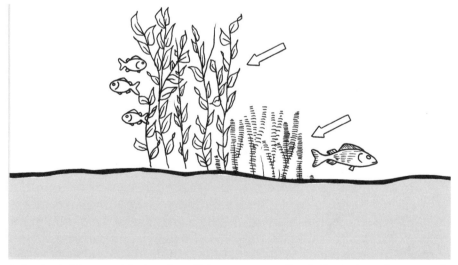

Animals of all types relate to edges. Fish are no exception. In the water, edges come in many forms. Edges can be found where two different types of vegetation meet or where vegetation ends.

The surface is an extremely important edge that gamefish use to trap their prey. Pictured is Charlie Simkins with a northern that came out of 15 feet of water to hit a Husky Jerk fished just under the surface.

areas they are attracted to gets you closer to areas fish may be using. **Edges are these areas! By fishing edges that are created by various elements in lakes and rivers, you will catch fish.**

Remember, many of the edges that are found in lakes are created by weeds. Unfortunately, they can rarely be seen as easily as lily pad edges. Nonetheless, they are just as important.

WEEDLINES: EDGES THAT CAN BE SEEN

During my seminars I often use a comparison between edges under the water and roads that we use above the ground. I like to think of edges as **the roads and trails used by fish in their daily travels around a lake.** Just like roads we use in our travels, not all edges in the fish world are used to the same degree. Some edges are dirt roads that are rarely traveled while others are the major freeways that are subject to heavy traffic. Naturally, it is these heavy traffic areas that we want to focus much of our attention on.

In my opinion, the "interstates" of the fish world are found at the deep weedline. The deep weedline is the area in a lake where light no longer penetrates to a sufficient level to sustain plant growth. Plants in lakes are no different than plants in soil. Without light, they can't survive.

Although I have done some snorkeling and have witnessed the deep weedline, I am not as familiar with it as a diver. I have had divers come up after seminars and describe the deep weedline for me. They described it as a low light area with an irregular outer edge. They also talked about how abruptly the deep weedline often ends. They did not find gradually tapering plant growth. It just sort of ends, forming quite a distinct edge.

Lily pads create very distinct edges that are easy to see and fish. There are many other types of edges under the water that we cannot see that attract fish.

The uniqueness of the deep weedline comes from all of the elements that are happening at that location. First of all, let's go back to the divers' statements about the low light conditions that are present here. For animals that can't blink or control the dilation of their pupils, this sounds like a pretty good place to be.

The deep weedline also has food. Insect life in the weeds attracts minnows which in turn attracts larger forage fish. Think of the times you have tried to troll a live bait rig with a crawler along a deep weedline. Perch and sunnies will often peck your bait to death, literally. Dinner is found at the deep weedline for many species of fish, big and small alike.

The deep weedline is also a congregating location for predator fish. At times you can use this fact to your advantage. There is one lake near my hometown that has very clear water. Because of this clarity, the deep weedline goes down close to 20 feet. Over the years I have learned not to get to this lake too early in the day nor stay too late in the evening. It never pays off.

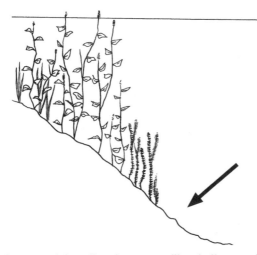

In my opinion, the deep weedline is the most important edge in a body of water. However, not all lakes have a distinct deep weedline. When it is present I like to think of this edge as the interstate of the fishing world. The deep weedline has all of the restaurants, rest stops, and motels that fish need in their day to day living. Fish it and you will be successful.

It seems that early in the day bass and northerns are scattered throughout the shallows looking for food. Along about 10:00 AM they start to gather at the deep weedline to spend the midday in comfort, lounging in the shadowy depths. This is the time of the day that I have my very best fishing. This is the time of the day the fish are schooled and bunched instead of spread out. It is not a matter of one here and one there. When you find fish, you find numbers of fish.

This midday philosophy works on more than just this one lake. It is a factor on many lakes, especially ones that are clear with a strong weed growth in deep water. Don't get me wrong, I am not saying it is poor fishing in the early morning and late evening. I am simply stating that with the conditions on this particular lake, midday is often the best time for finding concentrations of bass and northerns on the deep weedline.

Pictured here are my parents, Ralph and Jean, with a mess of northerns caught by trolling sucker minnows on the deep weedline.

Regardless of the water clarity and the types of weeds growing in your favorite lake, if you find a good deep weedline, fish it. **You will catch all bottom feeding species of fish found in that body of water at the deep weedline.** They will all use this deep weedline as a major staging and feeding area at various times throughout the year.

The deep weedline offers all of the elements that fish need for survival. It has restaurants, rest stops, lodging, and convenience stores. If you do nothing else but fish deep weedlines you will catch fish. I can't make it any clearer than that.

DEEP WEEDLINE SPECIFICS

Since the deep weedline is such a fish holding area we need to spend more time fine tuning this information. Fish that frequent the deep weedline don't just hang out on the very edge of it.

They make use of the area just above the weedline break as well as just below it. If you are going to go deep weedline fishing you have to keep this in mind.

You will frequently find situations where fish you are after will be holding extremely tight to the weedline, so tight that the person controlling the troll of the boat can put one side of the boat on fish while the other side remains virtually fishless.

Back in the days when there seemed to be more time, my brother-in-law, Gary Augustine, used to spend a considerable number of days with me in a boat. On one particular lake we fished, it was very common to find walleyes schooled tight to a distinct deep weedline. Because he could not see my electronics, he relied on me to tell him when it was safe to let his line down. My favorite trick was to position his side of the boat in the weeds and have mine perfectly arranged to be on the deep edge. As he was pulling in the weeds he snagged, I would be pulling in a fish.

I wonder if this has anything to do with the fact that he doesn't come to fish with me much anymore? Of course I would never consider pulling a dirty trick like that on him now!

Not all lakes will have fish this tight to the weedline. You have to consider the deep weedline to be an area that includes the weed growth just above it and the weedless area below it. If you are someone that enjoys catching bass, the area just above the weedline is often extremely productive.

If you are not into bass but prefer walleyes instead, you may be surprised at how many walleyes bass anglers hook as they are fishing bass in the deep weeds. Many times you will find that the bass are on the deep weedline, but the walleyes aren't. In this situation

Walleyes, such as the one admired here by Randy Amenrud, frequently make use of the deep weedline for travel and feeding. However, bass and northerns do too. Don't be surprised when you catch a mixed bag.

I usually try going somewhat deeper for the walleyes. Just how deep can depend on the lake. For starters, try going five to eight feet deeper. Walleyes and bass do not school together. If the bass are shallow, look for the walleyes a bit deeper.

One of my favorite weedline presentations is a live bait crawler rig. This outfit will appeal to a wide variety of fish including walleyes, bass, and sunfish. I am sure many of you are surprised to hear me mention sunfish. Usually we think of sunnies as fish that are located in shallow weedbeds but not in deep water. This is far from the truth. As a general rule, the biggest sunfish I catch each year come from the deep weedline and are caught while I am fishing walleyes.

On several occasions I have guided people that wanted to catch sunnies and I have been at a loss where to go. When this has happened, I go to the general areas I have caught them before and start trolling crawler rigs. My guests are usually quite confused by this strange sunfish method until we find fish. Once fish are located, anchoring is productive. The deep weedline is often home to the biggest sunfish in the lake.

EYES TO THE BOTTOM

It is not possible to learn everything there is to know about fish that are located at the deep weedline. After all, we can't see them and we can't see the weeds. To find out as much as we can about fish at the deep weedline we need to make use of our "eyes to the bottom."

I like to make use of both a flasher and liquid crystal graph. When trolling I use my liquid crystal for a more accurate reading of what is happening under my boat.

To locate fish on the deep weedline without some type of depth finder is nearly an impossible task. There simply is no effective method for doing this on a consistent basis. Sure, you can stumble onto an area that holds fish, but how can you find more areas that are similar if you can't see what is going on under your boat? Locating the deep weedline with the aid of electronics is easy.

With today's new age of electronics, the cost of decent depth finders has really come down. It is not necessary to have a depth finder that contains the latest in electronic gadgetry that will not only help you find fish but will teach you how to bid your bridge hand or play the stock market during moments when the fish aren't biting. A basic unit will suffice. I prefer to use a Vexilar flasher for locating areas that potentially might hold fish. Once I find a fishy area I will switch to some type of liquid crystal. I am currently using a Lowrance X65.

After fish are located, the liquid crystal helps me see size and quantity better than a flasher. Don't waste your money on a cheap liquid crystal that shows cartoon fish. These units are a very poor choice because of the low pixel count and poor definition. The cartoon fish you see may be weeds, minnows, baitfish, or several small game fish showing up as one big fish. **If you have the option, turn the cartoon fish off! You will get a more accurate reading of what is happening under your boat without the fish ID.**

Because edges are such fish magnets, it is an absolute must for average anglers to have a depth finder at their disposal.

INSIDE WEEDLINES: THE FORGOTTEN EDGE

One edge that we all too often forget and ignore is the inside weedline. This may be one of the most underutilized fishing areas in lakes where it occurs. Notice I said "where it occurs." Not all lakes have a good inside weedline.

The inside weedline is a shallow area where weeds stop growing. It is similar to the deep weedline except that it does not occur due to lack of

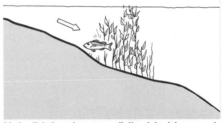

Not all lakes have a distinct inside weedline, but on lakes that do it is usually a forgotten edge. Quality bass and northerns can often be taken off of this important, underutilized area.

sunlight. It usually occurs because of a change in the bottom content, generally where the bottom changes from some type of fertile mud base to rocks or sand. Wave action may also have a bearing on this.

The inside weedline is a very limiting edge for fish. As long as they are in the weeds they are secure and safe. From this edge they can watch the open areas for feeding opportunities that occur. Feeding in open areas will take place in short spurts or after the cover of darkness. Remember, fish are the food source for many types of predators. The last thing a bass has in mind is being eaten by a blue heron while it gulps down a minnow. Predators of fish don't have to live in the water.

Because there is no security beyond the inside weedline it becomes a congregating and staging area much like the deep weedline. I have found the inside weedline to be a very productive area in the early morning and late evening low light periods. Wind can also help reduce the spookiness of these shallow water fish. **Fish positioned on the inside weedline are not resting. They are there to feed.**

The most productive day of bass fishing I ever experienced took place on the inside weedline. I was fishing a lake in the Park Rapids area of Minnesota with guides Kelley Cirks and Dick Winter. Although this day was cloudy and rainy, both Dick and Kelley claim that the fishing is nearly as good on clear days.

The bass, northerns, crappies, and large sunfish that we caught came from the inside weedline and the deeper weed area adjacent to it. We simply pitched 1/8 ounce jigs with four inch Culprit worms and caught fish after fish after fish. When the bite slowed, we scaled down to two inch grubs and caught a bunch more fish. When the day was done we had boated over 100 bass!

Utilizing the fishing opportunities of the inside weedline is not always possible because not all lakes have one. Besides, lakes that do have an inside weedline may only have it in certain areas. It will not be found all over the lake. In some cases it will be something you can visually see and fish accordingly.

Kelley Cirks (left) and Dick Winter (right) with some of the 100 plus bass caught off of the inside weedline.

CHAPTER SIX:
EDGES WITHOUT WEEDS

After the last chapter you probably get the feeling that I like to fish edges. Well, you're right, I do. But there is a reason for that. Throughout my fishing years on many different lakes (some with weeds and some without), edges have been one of the common denominators that I have used over and over and over again to locate and catch fish. Fish have not been found on every single edge that I have worked, but they are found on enough of them to make me a believer.

However, there is more to fishing edges than just fishing weed edges as outlined in chapter five. There is a lot more! **For every good weedline edge there is another edge that is not weed related.** These edges, for the most part, will be found below the deep weedline or found in lakes where there is not an abundance of weeds.

Once weeds are eliminated from the scene, structure takes on a different meaning. When fishing in and around weeds, the weeds themselves provide much of the actual structure that fish relate to. Away from the weeds you still have a lot of opportunity to locate and catch fish, and you still have plenty of structure. (Remember, structure is an area in an environment that is different from the immediate surroundings.)

On lakes without distinct weed edges diversity is still extremely important. Rock piles, transition areas where soft bottom meets hard, inlets and outlets, trees, docks, subtle depth changes, drop-offs, and humps are all examples of diversity on weedless lakes. These are the structure areas you need to focus on.

Fish species found on these weedless structure areas vary with depth and the type of structure. On lakes that have a walleye population, deep structure is a key. On lakes that do not have many walleyes, deep structure could hold bass, northerns and big sunfish. It may seem odd to see big sunfish listed as a species that uses deep, weedless structure, but it is true on many lakes. It depends on the food chain and ecosystem found on that particular lake.

DROP-OFFS

Non weed related, deep water structure takes on many forms. One of the most common elements is drop-offs. A drop-off is simply an area where the bottom changes depth very quickly in comparison to the surrounding area. This is a relative term and it is important to note that a drop-off in one area may look different than a drop-off in another. Let me explain.

Many Midwestern lakes offer very little in the form of structure. They may resemble a bowl when you look at them on a depth map. Sharp drop-offs are simply nonexistent on these bodies of water, yet they do have drop-offs. Drop-offs on these lakes will be gradual in comparison to drop-offs on other lakes.

On many of your basic bowl lakes there will be areas where the drop is faster than on the rest of the lake. This steeper drop may be a key for locating fish. This area of variation in drop-off may be all it takes for fish to want to relate to this area. Remember, fish do not do things by accident. The most dominant fish in the lake reside in areas that have the most to offer in terms of food and safety. A sharp drop-off puts predators closer to food and requires less effort in getting there and provides the safety of deep water close by.

A fast drop-off is not a quick fix to locating and catching fish. I know of several lakes that have great drop-offs yet contain few fish in those areas. I am sure it is the forage that is lacking.

On most lakes you will find a mixture of gradual and fast drops. The gradual drop on one lake may be steeper than the fastest drops-off on your basic bowl lake. **It isn't always the quickness of the break that attracts fish but a combination of conditions found in that drop-off area.** In another scenario you may find an area with a gradual drop that suddenly breaks to a very fast drop-off. This would definitely be a "structure area" I would want to explore further.

How fish relate to a drop-off depends a great deal on the species of fish found in your lake as well as the type of forage that is present. Just finding a drop-off certainly doesn't guarantee you will find fish along it. Besides, fish will often relate only to specific places along that drop-off. The diagram will help you understand more about specific areas along a drop-off that fish like to relate to. One of the critical areas of a drop-off is the lip. Walleyes, in particular, like to reside on lips associated with drop-offs.

FISHING THE LIP

Fish are often found in some very unusual places in a lake, sometimes where you least expect them. However, for the most part they have patterns that they tend to follow regarding areas in which they like to spend their time. When it comes to locating areas of drop-offs that fish will use, you have to focus on the lips.

The first important lip to examine is the top edge where the most prominent part of the

When you find distinct lips on drop-offs, work them over carefully. Predator fish, especially walleyes, like to lounge at these edges. During the summer months walleyes very often favor lips in the 25-35 foot range.

drop-off or break begins. Again, this will be somewhat determined by the lake and types of break you are dealing with. In some locations this top lip will be non existent because of the gradual break. In other situations, this top lip where the break begins will be very distinct.

This top edge is a real gathering point for fish. It is here they will stage to get ready for the next part of the journey to feeding areas. Fish found on this top lip are often aggressive and willing to bite.

Another important lip is the bottom edge. Not every drop-off will have this bottom lip. Many drop-offs simply have a gradual tapering without a distinct bottom lip. These bottom edges are often transition areas where the hard surface of a drop meets muck bottom. These bottom edges, or transition areas, can be excellent fishing spots.

Without weeds to hide in, fish become quite easy to pick up on your electronics. By cruising the edges of the drop-offs at a mid-range speed, it is very possible to locate schools of fish before you ever start fishing. You won't see every fish that is under your boat, but you should see some. Seeing a few fish is all you need to get started. Once you locate a few fish, check carefully for more.

Occasionally I will find large schools of baitfish in drop-off areas. When this happens I will definitely spend more time looking around for the predators that should be close by. I will usually drop a line and fish the area even if my electronics are not showing any larger fish. If fish are laying right on the bottom they can be difficult to observe on your electronics.

A TRUE EXAMPLE

I was just sitting in the office minding my own business one summer day when I got a call from an excellent angler and good friend, Corey Studer. I had asked Corey to call me when he had a day off from guiding so we could give his favorite Central Minnesota lake, Mille Lacs, a try. As it turned out the fish were biting and he was ready to go.

I was at the landing very early the next morning to meet Corey. His destination was the mud flats in the middle of the lake. For those of you that have never fished Mille Lacs, it has a series of mid-lake humps that are void of vegetation and top off at 23 to 26 feet. These mud humps are home to billions of insect larvae. These insects attract a variety of forage fish that prey on them. And of course, the predators, namely walleyes, follow the dinner bell to where the food is located.

On this particular day, we headed for a flat that had been producing well in recent days. With the aid of the GPS (Mille Lacs is 132,000 acres and a GPS comes in handy) we were able to motor right to our destination. It was not difficult to see fish on the liquid crystal graph. They were scattered along the top lip of the break. It wasn't until we dropped down to look at the bottom edge that we found the real concentration of fish.

Guide, Corey Studer, poses with a huge walleye that was probably seen before it was caught. It was part of a school that was hanging on the bottom lip of a mid lake hump.

It was very easy to hear the excitement in Corey's voice when he exclaimed, "That is a huge fish!" Over went the marker and out went our lines.

Now I can't tell you if it was the same huge fish Corey saw that bit his leech. All I know is Corey was soon fighting a monster.

Eventually, this monster walleye was led to the net and into the boat. It was a 30 incher guessed to weigh between nine and ten pounds.

Two important facts from this tale need to be pointed out. First of all, it was very evident that the fish we could see on the liquid crystal depth finder were either on the top or bottom lip of this drop-off. The big fish came from the bottom edge and was probably seen before it was caught. Second, there was a bit of a turn at this location. Most of the fish we found were holding very close to, if not on that turn. This is a classic example of fishing the "spot on the spot" that anglers talk about. It is also a classic example of using your electronics to find fish.

CHAPTER SEVEN:
TOO MUCH OF A GOOD THING

Some lakes have been described as a "structure angler's dream." In my opinion, these lakes are more of a nightmare than a dream. My reason for saying this is simple.

I know fish are attracted to areas of their environment that are different from the surroundings. As a general rule, the more "different" they are, the more attractive they are to fish. In many lakes there are probably dozens of potential hotspots you can identify either by looking at a map, by cruising the lake itself, or by guessing what is happening according to shoreline structure..

However, if you are at a lake that is nothing but structure, where do you begin? If the lake is nothing but a series of sharp drop-offs, which one will the fish be on? If the lake has points and food flats everywhere, how do you find the best one? These are tough questions without easy answers.

Many bowl shaped lakes have exactly the same problem only in reverse. With absolutely

Pictured are two contrasting lake maps. They both present similar problems with no place to begin your search for fish. One lake has too much structure and the other has too little.

no structure to concentrate fish, your task of locating them becomes much more of a hunt and peck. The fish are still there and they are still relating to structure, it's just this structure is much more subtle and difficult to find. **There is absolutely no doubt that lakes with limited structure are easier to fish than others.**

TACKLING THE OVER STRUCTURED LAKE

There is a lake in Central Minnesota called Clearwater that probably would fall into the over-structured lake category. I still remember how lost I was the first few times I fished on this body of water. It was so up and down it was very difficult to find a place to begin.

Logically, a lake map of this type of lake would be invaluable. However, I have not found this to be true. With so much structure to map it is an impossible task to get it all down accurately. Put yourself in this position. With structure everywhere, the best you can do is map out the most defined areas and do your best at the rest. Maps of over structured lakes are generally inaccurate.

There are ways to tackle an over structured lake. One very good method of learning a difficult lake is to glean information from somebody that knows this lake better than yourself. This may mean stopping at bait shops, hiring a guide, or visiting with other anglers at the landing. When it comes to gathering information at a landing, you have to play the situation right.

For the most part, anglers you meet at landings are relatively tight lipped. They are not interested in sharing information with someone that may steal their good spots. However, if you act like a fishing idiot (I can do this quite naturally on most days) and come across as no threat to the other anglers, they will often open up and share secrets.

It is crucial to ask the correct questions. **Don't** ask where they caught their fish. Instead, ask about depth, bait, method of fishing, and so on. Let them get a chance to realize that you aren't a threat to their fishing and they will tell you exactly where to go. What you are doing is gently playing to the ego and competitiveness of anglers. It is hard to pass up a chance to help someone that appears to be totally lost while expounding upon your own fishing skills.

ONE STEP AT A TIME

Once you actually begin fishing a complicated lake, **do not try to tackle the whole lake**. Instead, pick out a section of lake that you are going to learn and work on this area only. **Make sure that each time you go to the lake you fish at least one new area.**

This way you are slowly developing a list of spots that have potential as well as exploring new areas you can try on future trips. Gradually, you will learn which areas are good and which ones are worthless. You will also begin to see some fish location patterns. This will help you identify the types of locations fish prefer on this lake.

Fish in any given body of water are not all doing the same thing at the same time. If you are not meeting with success in one area, be sure to keep moving.

On lakes with countless places to fish, search out the more pronounced areas first. **If there are drop-offs everywhere you go, then look for a drop-off that has something different happening on it. Look for a drop-off with diversity.** This might be cabbage beds. Good weeds can be a real key for separating average spots from good spots.

Think back to the section on weeds, especially cabbage, and use this weed philosophy to help guide you to potential fish holding structure. If you have lots of cabbage, then you need to look for cabbage beds that are the thickest, closest to the drop-offs, and grow in the deepest water. Somehow you have to differentiate the very best spots from the poor ones.

KEEP MOVING

There are times when being super patient is the best strategy I can think of. However, there are other times when being patient and waiting for fish to come to you is the worst thing you can do. This is especially true on a lake that is loaded with structure. It is possible the area you are fishing so patiently may not hold any fish at all. **I believe that no matter what lake you are on, if you are not catching anything, keep moving! If you know what is not working, change it.** What have you got to lose?

Fish are not all doing the same thing at the same time. This is true on any given body of water. It is possible to have fish in a totally turned off mood in one area and biting like crazy in another, especially on lakes with tremendous structure. By continually looking for active fish you stand a better chance of being successful as well as standing a better chance of learning a difficult lake.

THE FISH FINDING GAME

I hate to pick on my brother-in-law again, but I can think of no better example than his. Besides, it is so much fun to give him a hard time!

In years gone by, I used to do quite a bit of guiding. I found that preparing for guiding was a time consuming but very interesting pastime. I never really knew just when the phone would ring and someone would want to fish, so I had to stay abreast of what was happening on area lakes. Due to the number of lakes that I fished, this was more than a full time job. It came down to what I call "the fish finding game." This is how it works.

This respectable northern was caught by Jay Adams while playing the "fish finding game."

When you are on a limited time budget to locate places to take clients fishing you cannot spend much time in one place. This means that every time you catch fish, you move. You are looking for as many places as possible that may have fish holding potential. You are not concerned with quantity. Worry about that when the clients are along. What you need is a long list of places that may have some action, even if it is limited.

What usually happens on days you have clients is that you get to the lake and your best two spots already have boats on them. The fish you thought you had going are getting caught by others. This is why you need to learn a number of potential spots. Once you

As much as I give my brother-in-law, Gary Augustine, a hard time, he is a very good angler. Here he is pictured with a "fish finding game" mixture that we kept for a photo and then released.

do develop a list of good fishing areas, **don't burn them out! Whether you are fishing alone or with clients, never stay in one spot so long that you literally catch everything there is to catch in that location.** Take some fish and then move on to other spots. This way you can come back to these areas another day and there will be fish there.

Back to my brother-in-law. I had been hired by his company to guide a group of business people on a lake with super structure. It was one of those nightmare situations where it was hard to tell where to fish. Gary was able to join me for the prefishing. With only a short time to prefish, it was imperative that we find as many fishing spots as possible. Much of the group would be on their own and would need instruction on where to fish.

There was only one way to handle this, the fish finding game. We spent two days trying dozens of different areas with different baits at a variety of depths. Once a game fish was caught, we marked it on the map and went on our way.

When Gary introduced me to the group, he shared his version of this horrible method of fishing I had put him through. He explained that he always believed you went fishing to catch fish. He described fishing with me as the opposite of normal. With me you moved as soon as you started catching fish and went to someplace where there weren't any.

Over the years, places that I have found through the "fish finding game" have saved me time and time again. It may seem like a crazy approach to fishing, but in reality, it makes a great deal of sense! It does help you learn lakes quickly.

CHAPTER EIGHT:
MID-LAKE HUMPS

I hardly go anyplace on a lake without my flasher running. There is a very good reason for this. Many of the very best fishing locations are not located on a map. They are small, uncharted humps and points that you stumble onto as you are traveling the lake. Without your depth finder on you would drive over these areas never knowing something unique was underneath you.

A classic example of this happened to me years ago. I had just purchased my first flasher, the old "Green Box." (This unit was standard angling equipment for many years.) My wife and I had been camping with our family on a small walleye lake near Alexandria, Minnesota. The tent had been cold so we had gotten up early to try our luck on walleyes. It wasn't any warmer on the lake than in the tent, but at least the sun was shining.

After trying several of the normal "milk run" spots with no success, we decided it was time to head back to camp for some breakfast and to check on the sleeping beauties. On the way back to the campground my flasher lit up as we went over a mid-lake hump I had never seen before. We immediately went back to investigate. Sure enough, here was a small, weed topped hump that had fish written all over it.

We put on a couple of fresh crawlers and gave it a try. Our Alumacraft went only a short distance before my wife hooked a good walleye. In the next half hour we caught several more walleyes on one little point off of the sunken island.

We have returned to explore this sunken island time and time again. The walleyes are not always there, but when they aren't the bass usually move in. We have also taken big sunfish off of this uncharted hump. The discovery of this small sunken island totally changed our fishing habits on this lake. This island became the "go to" spot. More importantly, it taught me to never turn off my electronics when I am traveling on a lake.

Another interesting fact about sunken islands is that once you find one, you often find others nearby. This was true of this spot. With a little investigation, we were able to find two more humps in the vicinity. Although we have taken many fish off of these other humps, neither of them has produced fish like the original discovery.

DIVERSITY

Without a doubt, some mid-lake humps are better than others. But why is this so? I have found the best mid-lake humps have something in common, diversity.

In an earlier discussion I talked about diversity as variety, where several things are happening in the same area or close to the same area. It is a group of "different" things together. The more different things, or variety that exists on a sunken island, the better chance you have of finding fish there.

The diversity factor includes many things.

SHAPE

If there is one quality that I would want a mid-lake hump to have it would have to be an irregular shape. An irregular shape is important to me because it gives me an area to start my search. An irregular shape gives the fish something out of the ordinary to relate to. Fish are attracted to things in their environment that are different.

Let's say that you have come across a sunken island that you think has some promise. By criss-crossing it with your locator you can see that there are some weeds on top and the edges drop off fairly well. You can also tell that this hump is pretty much as

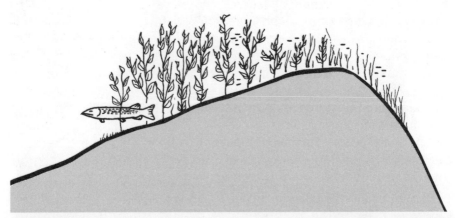

Any mid-lake hump should be fished. However, sunken islands with a little character will hold more fish. Use the shape of the hump to help you find a place to begin your search for fish. Round humps have no place to begin. Humps with points and corners have places the fish can relate to as well as places for you to begin your search.

round as it gets.

In my opinion, this is a poor bet. Don't get me wrong. Any sunken island has potential, but with one that is perfectly round, there is simply no place to start. You will have to fish the entire area to find just where the fish might be.

If the sunken island has some irregular areas such as a point, inside turn, or one high spot, you now have a place to start that has fish holding potential. You still may end up fishing the entire area, but I would put my money on the unusual aspects of the hump as the best bet.

Sunken islands will hold a variety of fish. Here my brother, Jay, is pictured with a sunken island bass that fell to a Culprit Burst Worm.

Many times when you are cruising a structure area such as this you will actually be able to see fish on your electronics. This certainly is helpful in determining where on the structure you should concentrate your efforts.

Not seeing fish doesn't necessarily mean there are no fish. Fish close to the bottom or in the weeds may not be visible on your electronics. The type of fish species you are after will also make a difference as to how visible they may be. Bass, for example, may not be as visible on your electronics as walleyes simply because they relate to weeds differently. Bass love to lay in the weeds with their noses pointed towards an opening while walleyes like to hang around the open areas below the deep weedline.

As a general rule you will get some feeling about the potential of a mid-lake structure just by how it looks on your electronics. The location of the hump in relation to other structure areas is also a consideration. A hump in total isolation may not be as productive as one in close proximity to other structure areas.

CHAPTER NINE:
THE SPRING MIGRATION

In the opening chapter of this book I stressed the fact that 90 % of the fish are in 10 % of the water. Without a doubt, this makes the whole fish finding scenario a real challenge. What makes it even worse is knowing fish move with the seasons. In this chapter we will focus on the spring to summer migration.

Each spring the warming of the waters signals an annual event is about to take place. This annual event, of course, is the spawn. Not all fish species spawn in the spring of the year, but for those that do it means they will be moving to a shallow location. **On most lakes, this shallow spawning area is some type of shoreline structure.**

The spawning ritual is not a sacred event reserved for predator fish such as walleyes and northerns. It is an event that the baitfish are focusing on as well. It is a well known fact that one of the keys to successfully locating good sized predator fish is to locate the areas that hold bait. Find the food and you will find the predators. If shoreline structure is where forage fish are spawning it only makes sense that shoreline structure is where early season fishing takes place.

NATURE'S WAY

Mother nature does not do many things by accident. This includes the spawning pattern of fish. Predators are the first to spawn. Not only are they the first to spawn, for the most part the predator spawn proceeds according to the food chain hierarchy. The most dominant species spawn first. (This does not hold true for muskies.)

For most lakes in the Midwest, the fish at the very top of

Spawning temperatures for Minnesota fish

Species	Temperature Range (F)
Northern Pike	36-37
Muskellunge	50-55
White Sucker	45
Smallmouth Bass	62-64
Largemouth Bass	62-65
Bluegill	67-80
Black Crappie	64-68
Walleye	38-44
Sauger	43-53
Yellow perch	45-52

From *Fishes of Wisconsin* by George C. Becker, University of Wisconsin Press, 1983.

the food chain is the northern. Northerns spawn very early in comparison to other fish. They will even begin their spawning before the ice is off of the lakes. This head start puts them in a position to remain at the top of the heap.

Since northerns are the first hatched they are also the first to grow. As baitfish and other fish species do their spawning thing, they become food for the young northerns that have grown enough to turn newly hatched fry into lunch.

This lunch scenario goes way beyond the young of the year. It controls the large adults as well. Early season is a time when many big northerns get caught. This is the time of year they move shallow to spawn and the time of year when their food source has moved shallow as well. If you want to catch a trophy northern, spring is a prime time to do it.

Walleyes are another major predator that rank high on the food chain hierarchy. Like northerns, they spawn early and have young of the year fish actively feeding as forage fish spawn.

RECUPERATION

Spawning is a strenuous activity for fish, especially the females. They are not ready to eat as soon as spawning is over. They need time to recuperate. This is one of the reasons early season fishing can be some of the most difficult of the entire year. Even if you do locate fish, they may not be very interested in biting.

Early season fish recuperate in the order in which they spawn. Early spawning northerns are going to be the first major predator fish to be rested and ready to bite each spring. Walleyes come next but are usually a week or two behind the northerns.

LOOK FOR THE MALES

Male fish are the first ones to become active after spawning. They will roam the lake in search of a very limited food supply. It is important to stress limited because **there is less forage in the spring than at any other time of the year.** (Most of the bait has been eaten.) If you are a walleye angler you know that male walleyes constitute most of the early season catch. Concentrating on them is your best option.

Hungry predators will not travel far from their spawning grounds. They will roam spawning areas until they find the forage base they are looking for. Again, it is important to remember this will more than likely be some type of shoreline structure.

Gradually, as the other fish species hatch, both the baitfish and the predators begin to spread out and scatter over the lake. This whole process takes time.

UNDERSTANDING THE FORAGE

Young of the year fish know they are in a very precarious situation. They know they are vulnerable to predation. They naturally respond to the cover opportunities that are available. For the most part, we are talking weeds again. But the weeds do more than supply cover and shelter to the host of newborn in the lake. They also supply food.

Small fish need small food. Small food is going to be found in the weeds in the form of zooplankton and phytoplankton. These microscopic plants and animals, along with insect larvae, are the primary source of food for young of the year fish. Weed growth is established in the warm, shallow water first which means the most abundant food is first found in the shallows. This is yet another reason to concentrate on the shoreline structure during the early season.

MOVING TOWARDS SUMMER

As the water warms and we progress into summer, weeds and food are gradually established in most areas of the lake. As a result of this, predators become established throughout the lake as well. Shoreline areas may still be good, but fish are starting to use off shore structure more and more. In fact, some off shore

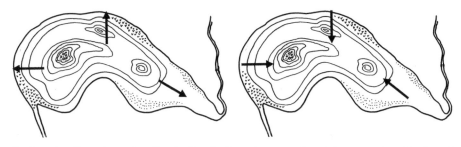

Each spring there is a migration to the shallows for spawning. After spawning fish do not move out to their summer haunts immediately. It takes time. Shoreline structure is the best place to concentrate your early season efforts.

areas will have the very best fishing on the lake. This is an indication that summer patterns are setting in.

It is during this summer period that I concentrate much of my fishing efforts on sunken islands and humps as well as deeper shoreline structure. Fishing mid-lake structure too early in the year can be a total waste of time, especially if there are no spawning areas close by.

SUMMARY

A lake needs time to come to life in spring. Concentrate your efforts in areas that are close to spawning grounds and in areas where there is food potential. This often means weeds both old and new. Follow the fish out to deeper water and to mid-lake areas as the food moves to those locations.

If you have the option to be flexible as to the specific lake you fish, consider yourself lucky. During this early season period lakes go through stages of activity at different times. Pick a lake that is active and avoid lakes that are not. As lakes get "hot" with activity simply switch

This dandy Rainy Lake northern came out of three feet of water. It was one of many early season fish we caught in the bulrushes of a shallow, weedy bay.

your efforts to places where fish are active. On a big lake the activity level of fish can vary greatly from one section of the lake to another. Mobility is one of the keys to success during this early season time period.

CHAPTER TEN:
THE SUMMER PATTERN

Without a doubt, summer is my favorite time to fish. It is not only a period of warm weather when a person can go fishing without dressing for winter, but it also is a period of stability in the lives of the fish. It is a period when fish seem to do about the same thing on a day to day basis. Sure, you have fronts come through that affect fishing to some degree, but as a general rule, you can catch fish of some kind nearly every day during the summer period.

One of the reasons for the stability in summer is the ending of the spawning period. The spawning period totally controls the lives of fish in terms of their location and feeding habits. This is true of fish that are spawning themselves as well as ones that are looking for food in the form of spawning fish. Fishing the spawn period can be an extremely productive time for catching, but it also can be a total hit or miss proposition.

Summer brings with it a whole new location strategy for fish. This location strategy is all about food and cover. The food that once was found primarily along shoreline structure has started to disperse throughout the lake. The weeds that were pretty much nonexistent early in the year have grown and now offer food and protection to young fish. This whole movement to the summer pattern takes time and is dependent on weather. The earlier the lakes warm up, the earlier the summer patterns take shape.

As weeds and food get established throughout the entire lake, the predator fish also get established throughout the lake. On lakes where they are found, mid-lake structure such as humps and sunken islands, are going to be very productive. It doesn't mean that you can't catch fish on shoreline structure. Shoreline structure can be as good or better than mid-lake structure if it has the correct ingredients. **The most important factor that determines fish location is food.**

FOOD FOR ALL

One drawback associated with summer is the availability of food. If there is one time of the year when the cupboards are overflowing, it is definitely summer. The weeds are flourishing, the young of the year fish are everywhere and very vulnerable, and life is good for predator fish. Predator fish **do not** have to work hard to get a meal.

There is a huge misconception by anglers that fish are always on the prowl in search of food. This is not true. Predator fish are very adept at finding and inhaling their meal. Fish do not work hard at eating, especially during this summer period.

I once viewed a short film that showed a bass in a tank being fed. Three minnows were dropped into the tank for lunch. The bass nonchalantly swam over to the minnows and then proceeded to eat them. In slow motion we could see the bass flare its gills and inhale these minnows in three separate strikes. These three strikes came in less than a second!

Fish do not nibble. They can inhale your bait, taste it, and spit it out in less than half of a second. We cannot react fast enough to match their reflexes. The next time you get a "nibble," you can rest assured that you missed that fish. Fish do not nibble.

SUMMER WALLEYES

If there is one fish that can frustrate anglers during the summer months, it is definitely the walleye. One reason for this is the abundance of food. Remember, it doesn't take fish very long to feed, especially when food is plentiful. The other reason is that walleyes have a preference for low light feeding. Walleyes have such a preference for low light feeding that your own timing for successful walleye fishing in the summer can be of great importance.

Walleyes have excellent low light eyesight. Baitfish do not. **It only stands to reason that if walleyes are to make the most efficient use of their energy they need to feed at periods when they have a distinct sight advantage over their prey.** During the summer this means early in the morning, late in the evening, and on cloudy or windy days. This may sound like a pattern you have heard about before. Fish don't do things by accident. They are opportunistic and take advantage of what nature gives them. **Feeding in low light is what walleyes are made for.**

As a walleye angler, you need to match your fishing times with the feeding times. Of course this is not always possible. We can't always pick our fishing trips around low light periods. Fishing during the day is what most of us do and yes, walleyes can be caught during the day.

SOMEONE IS ALWAYS HUNGRY

Cloudy, rainy days are often ideal walleye conditions. Walleyes have eyes that give them a distinct advantage over baitfish in low light. Windy days, cloudy days, dusk, and dawn are prime time for walleyes.

When was the last time you stopped at a restaurant to eat during a time of the day when it was not the normal lunch hour? Did you get served? Of course. Were other people eating? Probably. Fish, like people, are not all doing the same thing at the same time. Somewhere on the lake there is a fish or a school of fish that are in the eating mood. **Just because fish in one area of a lake are not turned on to feeding, it doesn't mean that fish everywhere are not feeding.**

It is true that walleyes are active during periods of low light or when the wind is blowing, but that does not make it impossible to locate and catch fish at other times. These midday fish may not be as aggressive as you would like them to be, but if you work at it you can usually find something they can't refuse.

A MIDDAY BITE

One of the most unusual walleye experiences I have ever had came at the end of a three day camping trip with my wife, Colette. We had spent the weekend at a lake where we normally found good walleye activity. This particular weekend we had caught nothing. Of course, we blamed part of it on the weather. (That is a great aspect of fishing. If you don't catch anything you can always blame it on the weather!)

We had experienced three days of 100 plus degrees and absolutely no wind. On the third day, after we had packed up camp and were about to head for home, my wife decided she wanted to go out fishing just one more time. It was nearly noon and the sun was as high in the sky as it was going to get. Reluctantly I said yes, but wondered to myself if she was suffering from too much sun.

Our first stop on the milk run of spots was a bust. This was no surprise. We had no bites nor did we see any fish on the electronics so it was off to the next stop.

As I backed the throttle down on the Mercury I saw the flasher light up with fish in deep water. My liquid crystal soon caught up to display a good school of fish. Our lines went down and we quickly had our first walleyes of the week-end. We followed the school as they traveled up to the deep weedline to feed. During the next 30 minutes we had spectacular fishing, and then they were gone.

Walleyes aren't the only fish that will get active during low light periods. Bass, such as the two held by Jerry Hayenga, will often become very active on days with a heavy sky.

We pulled back into the dock a little after 1:00 PM with a very impressive bunch of fish. I was shocked at the success we had just experienced. My wife was gloating as well she should. It just goes to show that the best time to go fishing is whenever you can. Somewhere on the lake there is apt to be fish that are willing to bite. The trick is to find them.

CHAPTER ELEVEN: WIND IS A KEY

I grew up on a widening of the Mississippi in a small town called Lake City. Lake City is located on the Minnesota side of the Mississippi and sits on a three mile wide and twenty mile long stretch of river called Lake Pepin. It was here that I had my first real introduction to fishing through my grandfather, Walt Copp.

Due to poor water clarity, there were very few weeds in Lake Pepin. Since our fishing was primarily from shore this was probably a good thing. Weeds can make shore fishing difficult. Honestly, I usually didn't think very much about the weeds except that occasionally I would snag one on my lure and have to remove it. I didn't really care for weeds all that much.

I never had any say where my grandfather and I were going to fish. I just rode in the car and got out when it stopped. I tagged along behind my grandfather until he started fishing and then I would fish too.

It wasn't until I was fishing on my own that I could make sense out of the areas my grandfather would choose to fish. Without weeds to hold and attract fish we had to find other structure items that would attract fish. Places that we would frequent were sand points, rock rip-raps, a manmade fishing pier, a floating barge open to public fishing, and windy shoreline. It may seem strange to see wind listed as a structure element, but in a way it can be.

THE IMPORTANCE OF WIND

The one factor that I did not understand in the early days of my fishing was the importance of wind. There were times when we would drive to a point, stop the car and watch the effects of the waves on the shoreline. Sometimes we would get out and fish and other times we would simply drive away and look for shoreline where the wind was better.

I remember one area in particular that we rarely visited unless the wind conditions were just right. Even as a boy I knew that a strong northeast wind was the key to catching fish at this location. It didn't happen right away either. It took several days of northeast wind to move the fish into this spot. We never went to this out of the way beach unless the conditions were just right and we never left this beach disappointed.

Wind is a critical aspect of fish location on lakes, especially ones that do not have much weed growth. If there are no weeds for baitfish to relate to then there are no weeds for predator fish to relate to either. On weedless lakes wind stirs up food and creates an opportunity for predators to feed. The fish migration that happens when the wind blows is not instantaneous. It can take some time for predators and baitfish to adjust to the conditions that are present. **Sometimes it may take hours or even a couple of days for fish, especially walleyes, to relate to wind conditions and wind-created currents in a lake.**

This factor is very evident on Leech Lake located in North Central Minnesota. On this particular lake fish move shallow and become active when the wind blows. If the wind is riling the water up off of Stoney Point and has been for a day or so, you can bet that there will be walleyes biting there. The longer the wind blows into Stoney Point the more time walleyes have to find it and the better fishing becomes. However, when the wind switches to a different direction, those fish will be gone in search of better feeding opportunities.

There seems to be quite a bit of controversy as to which side of a wind swept point is best for attracting fish. I have talked to anglers that will always fish the upwind side first and then the downwind side. I have talked to anglers that do exactly the opposite. **Regardless of which side anglers may prefer to fish first, they will all agree that it would be a mistake to avoid fishing a windy point. Most will feel that it would be smart to fish both sides of the point and probably the top as well.**

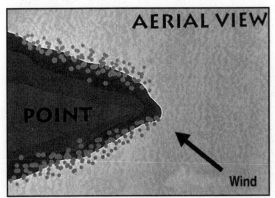

AERIAL VIEW

POINT

Wind

Without a doubt wind will turn fish on. Fishing in the wind is not always easy but it can be productive. When working a point in the wind be sure to cover the entire area. I like to start on the upwind side first.

WIND BRINGS FISH SHALLOW

One interesting aspect of wind is that it tends to bring fish shallow. This again has to do with feeding opportunities. Wind not only stirs up the food chain cycle, it also reduces the light penetration into the water. This is critical. As I mentioned in an earlier chapter, **low light situations give a definite sight advantage to predator fish. Baitfish become disoriented in low light conditions.**

Mille Lacs is a good example of a lake where wind brings fish shallow. Mille Lacs is a shallow, wind swept, 132,000 acre walleye factory in Central Minnesota. It is a lake where fish are caught shallow early in the year, caught deep in the summer months, and then return to shallow structure again in the fall.

When the wind blows on Mille Lacs fish will be found on shallow rocks no matter what time of the year. Certainly, the shallow bite is stronger early and late in the season, but walleyes can be caught shallow all times of the open water season if the wind is blowing.

Wind brings fish shallow and creates increased activity. This big walleye was caught in six feet of water under extremely windy conditions on Mille Lacs Lake located in North Central Minnesota.

Location on these shallow wind swept rocks is quite critical. I have nearly always had my best luck on the downwind side of the rocks. The upwind side will hold fish but in many situations the backside of the rocks is better.

WIND CREATED CURRENT

I remember a trip to Canada where I learned a valuable lesson on the importance of wind. We had been catching a good quantity of walleyes on several mid-lake humps and bars. Although the fishing was good it wasn't exceptional. During our stay we kept trying different locations in an attempt to locate the real honey hole.

We finally succeeded thanks to some help from another boat.

During our stay we had noticed a boat parked between two islands. After this party left for home we decided to check out the area they had been fishing. It turned out to be a pretty ordinary flat with depths ranging from 10 to 12 feet. It was then that we noticed the weeds all laying down from current. What we discovered was that the islands created a necked down area that channeled the force of the wind between them and thus created a current area. We also discovered that the walleyes were stacked in here thick!

The next day the wind was from a different direction and the fish were gone. The feeding opportunity that was holding them there had disappeared and so did the walleyes.

Wind often creates current that will help congregate fish. Pictured is Mark Stregge with walleyes that had positioned themselves in a necked down area and were taking advantage of feeding opportunities created by wind generated current.

There is a happy ending to this story. We took what we had learned from this situation and applied it to necked down island areas on other parts of the lake. If the conditions were right and the wind had been blowing from the same direction long enough for fish to find the minnows we were able to duplicate the pattern and catch walleyes in the wind generated current.

It was many years later that I again had a chance to utilize the fact that current will be channeled between islands. This happened in Ontario, Canada near Minaki. Sporting goods salesman, Mark Stregge, and I had only taken a couple of walleyes off of a wind swept rocky point when the action died. In our search for more fish I discovered a necked down area between two islands similar to the type we had fished years earlier. There was very little structure between these islands other than the current. The current was enough. The necked down area, combined with live bait rigs and leeches, produced walleyes until the wind switched.

WATER TEMPERATURE AND WIND

The first time I experienced the warm surface water and wind phenomena I was quite surprised. It was opening day for walleyes and the fishing was poor. I had been working the south end of a lake with tournament pro, Ron Anlauf. After a morning of absolutely no success fishing for walleyes, he decided to take his boat of anglers to the north end of the lake to test the bite up there. When we met up again that evening his story was very interesting.

The days prior to the opener had been sunny, but they had also been windy. What Anlauf discovered was that the wind had actually stacked up the warm water on the north end of this large lake. With water temps a full three degrees warmer on the north end of the lake the fish were more active there. Early in the season a few degrees can make a big difference in fish activity.

I have used this bit of information to my advantage many times since then. Warm water rises to the top of the lake and the wind pushes it along and stacks it up on shore. Using this fact can work to your advantage in some situations.

FLAT WATER

No matter how carefully we plan for our fishing outings, we cannot predict what the weather is going to be.

Some of the toughest days of fishing can come on clear calm days. Weather that is perfect for fishing is not always perfect for catching.

Sure, we could wait for just the perfect scenario of wind, tempera-ture, and clouds before we head to the lake, but we would only get fishing once or twice a year. Weather is seldom perfect. That is why most angers live by the philosophy of going fishing when-ever they can regardless of the weather.

There are times that you just plain have to make the best of the fishing situations you are dealt. Some days I do not want any wind when I am fishing, especially when I am bass fishing. I real-ly like the calmer days for my bass outings. I have better boat control than windy days and it is easier to see the subtle bites that you get on a plastic worm.

Actually, bass do not like real rough water, at least when they are shallow. Largemouth bass get seasick in rough water so they tend to avoid this situation. It is true that super quiet water will often drive them deep, but then this is the perfect time to work the dimly lit depths of the deep weedline.

I have had some of my very best crappie experiences on calm days. The flat water has allowed me to see the edges of the weedlines easier as well as locate pockets in the weeds and cabbage beds where crap-pies may be lurking.

If it is walleyes you are after, flat water will often chase them into the depths to reach a more comfortable degree of murkiness. This fact was really driven home to me when on a walleye trip with Randy Amen-rud and Fishing Pro-Mo's.

The first two days of this particular trip found the weath-er cloudy, windy, and overall gray. The walleyes were quite cooperative and were taken in many locations in water between 15 and 24 feet. And then came day three.

Ray Stommes displays a trophy walleye that came from over 40 feet of water on a clear, calm day.

On the third day of this trip we awoke to crystal clear skies and flat water. The walleyes we had been catching had moved....deep! The fish were still in the same areas they had been, but they were now in water over 40 feet deep. The difference in light penetration had dropped their depth by 20 feet!

SUMMARY

The effect that wind has on lakes is actually a book in itself. It is an extremely important part of any fishing outing. Knowing that wind gives a low light feeding advantage to predators is a fact that anglers should never forget. Wind also masks boat noise and makes it easier for us to get closer to game fish without spooking them.

We need to use wind to help pinpoint the location of fish, knowing that they will take advantage of the wind and actually move to favorable wind locations. This is especially true in lakes that do not have a substantial growth of weeds.

We also need to remember that on days when the wind is not blowing and the surface is calm, fish will react accordingly. Walleyes, in particular, will go deep or into the weeds to escape the light that they do not like. Bass will also go deeper or into the weeds but are not as affected by strong light as walleyes.

In short, wind is important. You can use it to your advantage to locate fish or use it to help you pick a fish species that may be more active in the wind conditions that you are encountering.

CHAPTER 12: LAKE MAPS ARE ESSENTIAL TOOLS

In the beginning of this book I referred to the adage that 90% of the fish are in 10% of the water. This magical 10% is scattered all over the lake and is frequently made up of small pockets that hold clusters of fish. It is certainly possible to have large concentrations of scattered fish, but for the most part you are hunting for small groups of fish.

Hunting for fish is often more difficult than regular hunting. Fish leave no droppings or trails behind for us to examine. You can locate areas you feel are good habitat for fish, but unless you actually see fish on your electronics or catch fish you cannot be sure they are there. Looking for fish is somewhat like scouting for deer with blindfolds on. We cannot see where fish are located or what fish are doing. This is why "scouting" for potential fish holding areas is important.

It may sound funny to hear the word scouting in terms of looking for fish, but it really isn't that unusual. If you were deer hunting you would certainly do some scouting before you put up your tree stand. You would not commit to hunting an area unless you knew deer were there. When hunting, we scout all the time in search of the right lay of the land for our stand site. Knowing the lay of the land helps us determine the daily movement patterns of deer. Knowing the location of bedding areas, food sources, and water is essential to smart hunting. Unfortunately, we can't do this with fish....or can we?

Unless you are a diver, it is very difficult to know exactly what lies under the surface of the water. The shoreline terrain will give up some clues, but for the most part studying the terrain of the bottom of a lake must be done with some type of sonar device, or maybe a map!

A fishing map can be worth its weight in gold. It can't always show you where fish are, but will often give you a very good idea where they aren't. It helps locate areas of a lake that will be void of fish and thus should be avoided by anglers as well. It helps you eliminate the unproductive 90% of the lake that does not hold fish. It also gives you clues about areas that might be part of the magical 10%.

Lake maps do help you find places to **begin** your search for fish. If you read maps correctly you get clues about where the magical 10% is located.

PICKING THE RIGHT SPOT

So exactly what are you looking for on a lake map? How do you find a fishy looking spot by examining a bunch of contour lines? How do you pick out areas of productive structure? There are some clues to follow.

Remember, fish are animals that relate to their environment in much the same way that other animals do. Because they live underwater and are not visible to the eye, it is much harder for us to know as much about them as other animals. We do know certain facts about their habitat preferences. We do know that food is a driving force in their daily movements and overall location. Knowing the food source for fish is no different than understanding the food source for deer or other animals that you are hunting. Security is also important and can be achieved through depth or cover.

Fish are attracted to elements in their environment that are different from the surroundings. This is what we call structure. When you examine a lake map, look for unusual things that are happening in an area. They might be points that stick out of a straight shoreline, an area with a fast drop-off that is surrounded with slow tapering bottom, an inside turn on a shoreline or point, or a rock pile in an area of soft bottom.

Sunken islands and mid-lake humps are classic spots that attract fish. When roaming fish come across a mid-lake area that offers food and security they take up residence. Some mid-lake humps will offer a great variety of structure elements themselves. These will be in the form of points, corners, and irregularities. It is these irregular spots that tend to hold the fish.

All of the information listed in the last two paragraphs is vital information for locating potential fish holding places in a lake. All of this information could come from a lake map.

THE REAL PURPOSE

It is impossible to look at a lake map and determine every place that fish are going to be. Maps are not designed to do that. Lake maps are designed to give you starting places to begin your search for fish. They are designed to help you eliminate unproductive areas. They are an extremely valuable tool for locating potential fish holding spots. They are a tool for helping you define areas of diversity. (Remember, many different species of fish are attracted to diverse areas.)

Once certain areas have been identified as 'potential' hotspots, you still must go out onto the lake and explore them to learn more. Electronics will give you a pretty good indication of what is happening under your boat.

Not every potential area that you pick out on a map is going to have fish. Maps are a beginning point. They give you a place to start your search and help you begin to eliminate areas in a lake that do not hold fish.

KEEP MAPS HANDY

Too many times I see anglers put their maps into storage after the initial trip to the lake. This is the wrong thing to do. Lake maps are more than just a beginning point. They are a tool that should be constantly updated. Very frequently you will find that there is a special little area on a piece of structure that tends to hold the fish

Not every good looking spot on a map is going to be a good looking spot once you are on a lake. However, maps do help you locate points and inside turns that will get you started. Areas, such as the ones I have circled, are key locations that I would explore first.

species you are after. These little "spot on the spot" locations should be drawn in on your map.

Frequently, the really good spots on a lake do not show up on a map. They are simply too small. Remember that a map is designed to be a general overview of the bottom contours, not a microscopic view of each tiny little detail. The little details are for you to discover once you are on the lake and fishing. To keep from forgetting where these little details are and what they look like you need to adjust your map accordingly.

KEEP THE LOCATOR RUNNING

As you travel about on a lake it is critical to keep that locator running. I prefer to use a flasher for my lake travels simply because it gives me more instant readings on the changes in bottom depth and hardness. Over the years I have found countless areas by accident that have turned out to be dynamite fishing locations. I would never have found these unmapped spots if I had not had my locator running. Once these uncharted areas are located, **mark them on your map so you can find them again.** If you are in open water and far from shore a GPS reading is helpful.

If you do find something unusual in terms of unmarked structure and it does not hold fish, mark it on your map anyway. Just because there are no fish on this structure today does not mean that there never will be fish on it. It never hurts to have one more place to check on your milk run of spots.

SUMMARY

Lake maps are an incredible tool for anglers. Although they are never going to be perfect, they give us a basis for a planned attack on a lake. They eliminate places that don't hold fish and help us pinpoint potential fish holding spots. They allow us to focus in on structure elements that may need further exploring. **Lake maps greatly reduce the amount of time it takes to learn a lake and locate fish.**

Fish do not leave tracks or trails for us to zoom in on when we go to the lake. Maps are the best tool that we have available to speed up the fish finding process. Going fishing without a map is like going hunting with your eyes closed. It is like dri-

Marking the exact location of "hotspots" on your map will help you develop a "milk run" of spots to try on your next outing. Be sure to redraw areas that are not accurate and add your own depth readings if they vary from the map. NOTE: If you are fishing lakes in Minnesota or Wisconsin there is an internet site where you can download lake maps and print them out. The web site is fishmap.com or call 1-800-450-2108 for more information.

ving cross country in your car without a road map or road signs.

Learning a lake is a never ending process. The extended use of a map is part of this learning process. Maps should be redrawn and remarked according to the information that you learn on your fishing outings.

You may have the best bait, the finest rods and reels, the fastest boat, and the most patience, but if you do not have a map that helps you locate places to fish, the rest can become meaningless. **Maps and depth finders are essential tools for successful angling.**

CHAPTER 13:
REMEMBERING TO THINK

I will always remember a comment made by outdoor writer, Art Perry, during a radio interview I did with him. We discussed the fact that anglers tend to spend very little time thinking about what they are doing when they go fishing. Art described it well. He suggested that once anglers get to a lake they unscrew the tops of their heads, take out their brains, set them on the dock, and **then** go fishing.

The worst part is, there is some truth to this! I am guilty of doing this myself. Many times I have been on the way home and realized what an idiot I had been for not having tried some different techniques. For some reason brains are often in neutral when we are fishing. This can be remedied with a little preplanning before one ever gets to the lake.

PLAN FOR MOBILITY

I am amazed at the number of times I see anglers live and die on one lake, or in one spot on a lake for that matter. On one particular ice fishing trip I ended up fishing next to a person that had this "wait em out" mentality.

There are times when waiting for fish to come to you is a good option, but you must be reasonable about how long you wait. Being willing to move to where the fish are is an important part of success.

As I hopped from hole to hole looking for active fish, he sat in one spot the entire time. I probably spent an hour in this part of the lake before I decided to move on. As I was packing up he came over to visit.

Naturally, he wondered if I had experienced any success, which I hadn't. I told him I not only didn't catch any fish, but I basically could not find any fish showing up on my Vexilar. The fish simply were not there. He agreed. He had been there all day and had not had a bite.

This probably isn't all that unusual except that he went on to say that he had fished the same holes the day before and hadn't had a bite then either. I must have had a bewildered look on my face because he then volunteered, "They have to bite sometime so I'm going to wait them out." Not me! I went to a different lake and caught a mess of sunnies and crappies.

This true story is not all that unusual. I have seen anglers sit in a boat all day with little success, yet too stubborn or too lazy to move or try something different.

FISHING MEMORIES

One of the very worst ruts that anglers can get into is fishing 'memories.' This happens when we go to a certain lake or to a specific spot an a lake and just sit there. While we are there and not catching a thing we comment about "a bad day of fishing is still better than a good day at the office." And then we start telling all of the "remember when...." stories. Yes, this lake or par-

ticular spot was maybe very good in the past, but **if what you are doing today is not working, change it!**

Lakes change just as structure on lakes change. Due to poor spawn seasons, high baitfish populations, fluctuating water levels, or run off, lakes will go through good and bad cycles of productivity. If the lake is hot and producing, by all means go

Not all lakes are doing the same the same thing at the same time. One lake can be dead and another one a mile away can have an active bite. It is not uncommon for us to hit three lakes in one day as part of this searching effort. By being willing to move to search out active fish you greatly increase your chances.

there. However, if conditions on that lake are not favorable for creating a good bite, go somewhere else. Plan this second or third lake into your fishing outing.

I can't tell you the number of times I have bombed on the first lake of the day but found the second or third lake to have very active fish. Sometimes you have to face the fact that you can't make fish bite. Go to a lake where the action is occurring.

Lakes are not all doing the same thing at the same time. Different water temperature, different weed growth, or different lots of things will control the activity level of fish on a lake. Take advantage of this fact and move to where the action is.

KEEP THINKING

After you have caught fish in a specific spot on a lake, have you ever stopped to wonder just what it was that made fish want to be in that location? What were the fish relating to? Was it a specific type of weed, was it baitfish, was it an inside corner, or a point?

Fish don't do things by accident. They are where they are for a very good reason. If possible, you need to learn what that reason is so you can locate similar areas where fish can be found.

SUMMARY

If you really want to be successful you must think and make plans for your fishing. Too many times we disengage our brains during our stay at the lake. By making plans before you get to the lake and then by following through with them,

Big bass, such as the ones displayed here by Neil Welman, often come because of effort and planning. Being at the right spot at the right time helps, but so does a little common sense.

you increase your odds of being successful on a more consistent basis.

Keep moving. Don't spend the whole day on one piece of structure or at one depth if it is not working. Fish many different lakes. Go where the fish are active. You may be doing everything right, but if the fish are shut down on your lake, fish someplace else. **Lakes are not all doing the same thing at the same time.**

Think about the areas that you do catch fish. Try to figure out why the fish are where they are and then try to duplicate this scenario in other parts of the lake or on other lakes. You will be surprised at how consistent some patterns can be.

CHAPTER 14: LIVE BAIT RIGS

Without a doubt, anglers have their own preferred methods and styles of fishing as well as preferred fish species. This is exactly as it should be. With a leisure sport like fishing, we should be able to pick and choose how we want to fish and what we want to fish for. However, when it comes to choosing what you are going to fish with, live bait is tough to beat.

Earlier in this book I did a short section on fish senses. They have the same basic senses that we do. However, water and air do not transmit information in the same manner so there are some major differences in how information is received and interpreted.

In order to catch fish we need to somehow get them to take a bait into their mouth. The only way fish put something in their mouth is when they think it is food. This means **the only way to catch fish is to make them think that our offerings are something that is really good to eat.** This is not always an easy task.

Fish eat by flaring their gills and sucking food into their mouths. This only takes a fraction of a second. Fish can inhale a bait, taste it, feel its texture, and spit it back out faster than our reflexes can react.

In order for us to catch fish we have to have them hang onto the bait long enough for us to know they are there and set the hook. This process can sometimes take a second or longer. (Successful anglers are often the ones that detect bites easier and set the hook faster than others.)

Live bait encourages fish to hang onto bait longer. **Live bait is often the easiest and most successful method of catching fish that there is.** This is not a hard and fast rule, but is a generality. Live bait appeals to more of the fish's senses than anything else we can use. There are certainly times when artificials will out-produce live bait, but for average anglers, live bait should be part of their fishing strategy.

LIVE BAIT RIGS

When it comes to fishing with live bait I use a live bait rig of some sort more than anything else. Over the years I have found that this system is about as simple as it gets and will catch a variety of fish in many different situations.

The live bait rig, or Lindy Rig as it is sometimes called, works with several baits including leeches, crawlers, and all sizes of minnows. With live bait you can work variations that will match the species, the location of the fish, or the mood of the fish. These variations include heavy snells for northerns, light snells for walleyes, spinners, floaters, and weedless hooks.

The basic concept of the live bait rig is to have a sliding sinker that is heavy enough to get you down to the bottom and a snell that separates your bait from the sinker. Snells can be bought or hand made depending on your preference and what you are fishing for.

One reason live bait rigs are so successful is the sliding sinker. While you are drifting, trolling, or casting your live bait

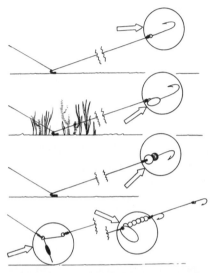

Sinkers come in a variety of shapes, sizes and colors. I prefer slip sinkers that I can change without having to cut and retie.

Live bait snells are often thought of as walleye tools, but they do not have to be just for walleyes. By changing the pound-test line of the leader and by using different hook sizes, live bait rigs can work for many species of fish. Diagram 1: A straight snell and sliding sinker is simple yet effective. Most leaders I use are about four feet long, but under certain conditions I will use leaders as long as 12 feet. Diagram 2: Floating jigheads allow you to get your bait up off of the bottom and above weeds. They also add color. Diagram 3: I frequently add a colored bead or two to my snell. There have been times when this colored bead has saved the day. Diagram 4: Bottom bouncers and two hook crawler spinners can be real walleye killers during the summer months. You do not want super light line for these snells and you do want to cover water quickly.

rig you are waiting to detect some type of bite which indicates that a fish has taken your bait. However, because your line restricts the movement of your bait, the entire bait is usually not inhaled successfully by the fish.

With a sliding sinker you are able to feed out extra line to give fish time to reposition the bait and take the whole thing in their mouths. Without the line being able to slide through the sinker the fish would have to drag the sinker around with them. Dragging a sinker may not seem like a big deal, but to a fish, this extra weight is not natural and it may decide to spit the bait out.

LENGTH OF THE SNELL

Live bait snells can be purchased in nearly any tackle store. The problem with store bought snells may be the length. The length is frequently too short for much of the walleye fishing that snells are purchased for. I believe over the counter snells are usually tied with too heavy a line as well.

Fish get conditioned to certain presentations. They somehow learn that danger is associated with unnatural events they see in the water. Sinkers are one of those items. As a sinker drags across the bottom of a lake it kicks up silt, mud, and sand. This disturbance does help get the attention of the fish, but it also warns them that the bait following along behind isn't quite natural. This is where a longer snell is helpful.

By using a longer snell you are able to put more separation between the sinker and the bait. This separation seems to help conditioned fish bite a little better. Snell length is also important for another reason.

Active fish frequently rise up off of the bottom of the lake. You can easily see this with your electronics. A long snell will present your bait further from the bottom than a short snell. A long snell will allow your bait to rise higher and get in front of the fish that you want to catch.

This can be extremely important. Fish have eyes that are located towards the top of their head. They see things above them better than they see objects below. You never want to be dragging your bait underneath fish. You always want to be at their level or above them. Fish will readily rise higher to take a bait but will rarely go lower to take a bait. When you drag a bait underneath a fish, that is a fish that you will not

catch.

So what exactly is the correct length of snell to use. That depends on the situation. In most cases a three to five foot snell will suffice. However, there have been times when I have had to resort to ten to twelve foot snells to catch fish. I prefer shorter snells if they will produce.

FLOATERS

I remember when floating jigheads first came out. My introduction to them came as a spectator. Fishing is not a great spectator sport. To sit in a boat and watch someone else catch one walleye after another on floating jigheads when you don't own one is an experience not easily forgotten. I have since become a real believer in floaters.

This walleye was caught by using a very long snell. Long snells will get your bait up off of bottom and will separate your sinker from your bait.

In my opinion, floaters work for several different reasons. First of all, they get your bait up off of the bottom where it is easier for predators to see. A six foot leader and floater will probably get your bait three feet off of the bottom provided you are trolling slowly. If you are trolling fast, the resistance of the water will bring the floater lower.

I also like floaters because they add color. I am not always sure how important color is, but I do know there have been days when fish were caught on one color only. This 'one color phenomena' is the exception and not the norm. Don't get totally hung up on color.

The third reason I like floaters is that they keep me out of the weeds. Many times I find myself fishing the deep weedline. The deep weedline is not perfectly straight and by trolling it you will occasionally bump into weeds. By using a floater I have fewer weed problems. If your lake has moss growing on the bottom, a floater is extremely helpful in keeping you above this annoying greenery.

The last reason I like floaters has to do with movement. Floaters give your bait more vertical as well as horizontal movement. Troll your bait in shallow water sometime to see how this works. Certain styles of floaters will give you more movement than others.

MORE THAN JUST WALLEYES

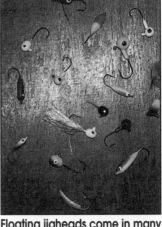

Floating jigheads come in many different shapes, styles, and colors. They are very effective and should be part of your fishing arsenal.

I like to catch walleyes as much as the next person, but at times I find myself on a lake that doesn't have walleyes or has walleyes that are not biting. This is when I will rig up a heavy mono leader with a floater and troll sucker minnows. If the lake has a good deep weedline, that is where I will focus my efforts.

I like to tie my own northern snells. I use 25 pound-test mono and a variety of hook styles including large floaters and weedless hooks. Northerns will cut mono leaders from time to time, but you will still out produce steel leaders four to one.

Sucker minnows are a great search tool for my fishing. I will catch northerns, bass, and an occasional walleye on sucker minnows. Once I find an active school of fish I can work them in a different fashion if I so choose.

I am sure that some of you cringed when I mentioned bass on live bait rigs. I fish live bait rigs a lot for bass. Once I find them I can then fish them with plastic worms or some other artificial. It is hard to beat a plastic worm for bass. However, there is something about small sucker minnows that bass can't resist.

CARE OF BAIT

Regardless of what type of live bait you are using or how you are using it, you must take precautions to keep it fresh.

Fresh, active live bait will nearly fish itself. If you are using leeches or crawlers, keep them in some type of cooler with ice. Sun is a real enemy of leeches and crawlers. If they are left in the sun for even a short time they are toast.

Minnows can also be a problem. During the summer months when the water is warm, minnows need a lot more oxygen to keep them going than when the weather is cool. You can greatly extend the life of your minnows by adding some ice to the water. I also use a portable aerator that adds oxygen to the water. This nifty gadget keeps a bucketful of minnows alive all day. It runs off of a six volt lantern battery and will run for days on the same battery.

 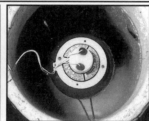

If you are going to fish with live bait, you must keep it fresh and lively. Keep your leeches and crawlers in a cooler. For minnows, a good portable aerator is worth its weight in gold!

SUMMARY

Live bait rigs are wonderful fishing tools. They are an effective way to present the "real thing" to fish. They are also versatile. With live bait rigs you can use floaters, spinners, weedless hooks and the like. They work for a variety of species but are extremely effective on the finicky walleye. If used with good "lively" bait, these rigs are hard to beat.

One last comment on live bait rigs has to do with mobility. It is difficult to find another presentation that will allow anglers to search for fish as effectively as you can by trolling or drifting live bait rigs. By continually moving until you find fish, you increase your chances of success. Live bait rigs and mobility go hand in hand.

Here is a trick to try. Before heading to the lake put your crawlers in water and ice. The crawlers will swell to enormous size plus you will not have all of the messy bedding to hassle with.

CHAPTER 15:
JIGS AND SLIP BOBBERS

There are more ways to present live bait than with a live bait rig. One of the most popular methods of presenting live bait is with a jig. In reality, a jig is not all that different than a live bait rig except that your sinker is attached to the hook and that you, as the angler, are responsible for most of the action of the bait. Often times, rigs and jigs can be fished interchangeably with equal success. There are times, however, when a jig is really the only way to go.

Jigs have a real advantage over other presentations when you are fishing rocks and snags. Rocks are real tackle eaters. Jigs allow more control over your bait when the bottom is snaggy. They allow you to hop, skip, and swim your lure over the bottom much more effectively than you could do with a rig. With a jig it is easy to drop it down, test the bottom, and then lift it back up to stay at the correct depth. Jigs simply give

A jig and minnow is one of the simplest yet most effective combinations possible. You can never be sure what you will catch on this combo. It appeals to a variety of fish.

you more control over the depth of your bait.

How you present your jig will have a lot to do with the number of strikes you trigger. The extra action imparted by the angler into the jig will often induce a strike where a more subtle presentation would not. For this reason there are times when hopping and skipping your jig can be very important. On the other hand, there are times when a slow swimming action is clearly the best. A slow swimming retrieve works great in cold water or on days with a tough bite.

Jigs are extremely versatile and can be used effectively in river current as well as in lakes. Jigs do not have to be fished with live bait, but live bait seems to help. Live bait adds scent and a visual appeal to many jigs. I have found that the condition of your bait is less important when it is fished on a jig. Dead minnows often work as well as live ones. Instead of using a whole crawler, try using half of one. A medium sized leech can be as good as a jumbo when fished on a jig.

Jigs are often thought of as a cast and retrieve lure. Although this works well, jigs can also be trolled effectively. This trolling can be done with or without live bait. If I am trolling a jig without live bait I will definitely have some type of plastic body on the jig. I feel plastic gives more action and feels more like food when a fish does take it in its mouth. Twister tail grubs and plastic worms are my favorite plastics to put on jigs.

Picking the correct weight and style of jighead is a critical part of successful jig fishing. As a general rule, I feel anglers use a jig that is too heavy for the location or depth they are fishing. An important feature of jigs is their ability to trigger fish as the jigs fall. Fish in general are real suckers for falling baits. Small, lighter jigs will fall slower than larger jigs and will stay in front of fish and in the strike zone longer. **Use the lightest jig possible for the conditions you are fishing.** On a river this may mean 3/4 ounce. On a lake it may mean 1/16 ounce.

Jighead styles and shapes are also a consideration. Most of the time your standard round head jig will work fine, but there are situations when something different is better. If you are fishing in weeds a weedless jig works great. A jighead with the eye at the very end will catch less weeds than a round head. Sometimes jigs that stand up will out produce other varieties.

Jigs and jig bodies certainly come in many shapes and forms. There is nothing wrong with mixing and matching. Tipping jigs with leeches, crawlers, and minnows will increase your catch. Putting a chunk of plastic on the shank for added color doesn't hurt either.

There is also the matter of hook size and shank. You do not want to use a jig that has the hook point even with the eye on the head. When this happens the eye actually acts as a hook guard and keeps the hook from lodging in the mouth of the fish. This is especially true of smaller jigs. This problem can be easily rectified by opening the curve of the hook so that the tip extends beyond the eye. I will usually bend a slight twist in the hook as well so the point of the hook is offset from the eye.

Short shanked jigs are often preferred by anglers using live bait. The short shank puts the bait closer to the head of the jig.

Others like the longer shank because they can add a piece of plastic on the shank or can go through the mouth of the minnow and hook it through the back. Most jig anglers that I know carry a real variety of jigs to meet different fishing conditions.

The bottom line: Jigs are an extremely versatile and effective angling tool.

SLIP BOBBERS

I am a real fan of slip bobbers because they absolutely work great. If you do not currently use them as part of your fishing arsenal, you are missing out on a great opportunity for catching fish.

No matter where you are fishing or what you are fishing for, there are times when you have a school of fish that is so tight to structure that you need to anchor to adequately work those fish. This is the slip bobber's moment of glory! There simply is no better way of getting your live bait in front of schooled fish than with a slip bobber.

It is true that there are some people that do not like to fish a bobber and there is nothing wrong with that. However, there are times when the bobber is the only way you are going to catch anything! Here are some scenarios where slip bobbers work great.

WHEN TO USE A SLIP BOBBER

I have found situations where fish were located tight to a weed wall. Penetrating this weed wall with live bait jigs and rigs is nearly impossible. By using a slip bobber you can fish the outer edge of the weeds and wait for the fish to come to you. Fish set up inside the weeds with their noses looking out. A tantalizing bait hanging in front of them eventually gets their attention.

Suspended fish can be

Illustrator, Larry Mattocks and his son Chris, show off a couple of slip bobber northerns.

worked well with a slip bobber. We once taped a television show where we fished trout 50 feet down in over 100 feet of water. A good bobber stop that will slide into your reel will allow you to do this. It is easy to fish deep water with a slip bobber if you are set up properly.

On many occasions I have had inexperienced anglers in my boat. They have ranged in age from six to 83. Trolling or casting with inexperienced anglers is darn near impossible. This is where slip bobbers come into play. Novice anglers have little trouble fishing with slip bobbers.. There are no long leaders to worry about, just the short distance between the split shot and the hook. A bobber also allows anglers to see when they have a bite.

Kids of all ages love to fish off of docks. Often times you will encounter such deep water off of the dock that a standard bobber and leader is impossible to cast. Slip bobber to the rescue! Simply set your bobber stop at the desired depth and cast away. Fishing deep water from docks or shore is very feasible with a slip bobber.

There is a walleye lake in Minnesota called Mille Lacs that is a perfect place for slip bobbers. When the wind blows on Mille Lacs the walleyes move up onto shallow rocky reefs to feed. Fishing these rocky reefs in heavy wind is very difficult. However, anglers have found that slip bobbers allow you to anchor off of the reef and float your bait exactly in the fish zone with no worry about spooking these shallow fish.

One of the added little things I like to do when fishing walleyes

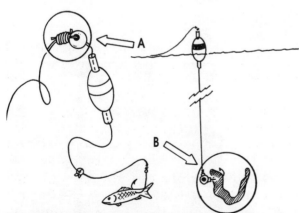

with slip bobbers is to replace the hook with a small jig. This small jig seems to work extremely well. It adds a weight at the business end to keep your bait deep as well as adding some color for attraction.

Slip bobbers also work well after dark. Tackle compa-

Slip bobbers are easy to use and are very effective. They are especially great for kids and inexperienced anglers.
A. Bead and bobber stop   B. Small Jig

nies, like Blue Fox, make lighted bobbers that work great in darkness. The small lithium batteries last just short of forever. These bobbers can also be used in the daylight without the light on. Being able to see your bobber after dark has really opened up a new world of night fishing for many anglers. By the way, if you have never tried night fishing with a bobber for walleyes, it works.

Slip bobbers can be used for any species of fish. They work equally well for panfish, northerns, and walleyes. **If you are using slip bobbers for northerns, do not use a steel leader. Use a heavy mono leader instead.** I prefer to tie my own

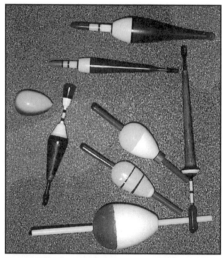

Slip bobbers have been made for every fishing situation imaginable. They even have lighted ones that will work at night. Many styles have been designed to be added or removed from your line without cutting and retying.

out of 25 or 30 pound-test-line. Steel leaders stifle the movement of your bait and tend to scare fish. You may have a northern that will occasionally cut your heavy line, but in the long run you catch far more fish.

SETTING THE HOOK

Many anglers struggle with the proper hook setting technique for slip bobbers. If you are using a bobber in deep water it is very easy to set the hook too soon. The fish that has taken your bobber down may not be swimming away from you as the line indicates. It is possible that there is a huge bow in the line and that the fish is actually swimming towards you and not away.

If you set the hook too early when using a slip bobber you run the risk of setting the hook on nothing. The best rule to follow for setting the hook is this. **Once the bobber is down, reel in slack line until you actually feel fish. Then set the hook.** Feeling fish before you set the hook will eliminate the tendency to set the hook too early.

CHAPTER 16: ARTIFICIALS AND CRANKBAITS

I have to admit that I am guilty of avoiding artificial lures more than I should. One of the fishing ruts that I get caught up in is live bait. Live bait is hard to beat, but there are times when artificials are really the only way to go.

When we look at the whole spectrum of artificials, there are really a lot of choices, probably too many choices when it comes right down to it. With so many lures to choose from, how can you know which one is best? The fact of the matter is, **many artificial lures are designed to catch anglers more than they are designed to catch fish.**

The artificials that I am going to focus on are the crankbait or minnow type artificials. These lures represent minnows to fish. They not only appeal to their sense of sight but also appeal to their sense of feeling because of the baitfish-like vibrations they send out. These water displacement vibrations, or wobble, are the key difference between many artificial cranks that work and many that don't.

STICK WITH THE BASICS

In and effort to not only save you a great deal of money, but a great deal of fishing frustration as well, I have one suggestion. Stick with name brand baits. There are more artificials out there than you can possibly carry in your boat. There are more artificials out there than you can use in a summer of fishing. So unless you have a very specific purpose in mind for some new fangled 'gitter-getter,' spend your money on a few of the tried and true lures and forget the rest. Personally, I stick with the Rapala family of lures. If the fish aren't hitting them, I know that it is not because of a poor quality bait. If I am using inferior quality baits I can't be sure.

IT'S IN THE WOBBLE

Minnow type crankbaits come in many different shapes and sizes. It is these shapes and sizes that we need to pay attention to when we are fishing. Different fish have preferences for different types of baits. This preference can actually change with the seasons.

If you are a walleye angler, you need to know that walleyes prefer a slower, looser wobble than bass and northerns. For this reason baits shaped like a slim minnow work better than baits shaped like a pregnant sunfish. This preference also has to do with matching up the lure to the type of prey walleyes are looking for. Walleyes don't like to eat sunfish. They have the wrong shaped mouth to devour sunfish. Bass eat sunfish. That is what their bodies are designed for. That is nature's plan.

In my opinion, crankbaits are underutilized by most anglers, including myself. Crankbaits not only tend to catch bigger fish, such as this nice bass held by Neil Welman, but they will frequently work when nothing else will.

In the spring of the year and again in the fall, slim, Rapala style minnows will usually out produce other varieties. During the cold water periods, minnows swim slower. They give off a slow wobble into the water as they move along. Minnow type lures that duplicate this slow, loose wobble will produce better than fast wiggling minnow baits.

During the summer months this may not be true. It is during this time of the year that I have had great success with the Shad Rap. This is probably my favorite crankbait of them all. It just catches fish. This is due to the fact that it comes in several sizes and colors, works equally well at fast and slow speeds, can be worked at different depths, and is easy to fish.

If you are someone that prefers fishing bass and northerns more than walleyes, you may want to try the fatter, chubbier style crankbaits. These lures have a whole different wobble than the slim minnow style. They give off heavy vibrations that attract bass and northerns more than walleyes. They are often at their best when retrieved very fast.

CHOOSING THE CORRECT SIZE

Making a decision regarding the best size to use is a dilemma crankbait anglers must face. One consideration is the fact that **fish can comfortably eat baits that are one third the size of their body.** Forage of this size is a good meal. By eating larger forage predators are also ensured that they will gain more energy from the food they eat than the energy they expend in chasing it. This is why the old adage of big fish big bait is so true. Big fish eat big food. Little fish eat little food.

There is a catch here. It is not that simple. By using very large baits you eliminate the possibility of catching smaller fish. Small fish cannot eat big baits yet big fish can eat small baits. If you are in doubt, smaller is better than larger in most situations. If you only want large fish, stick with large baits.

Forage is one other factor that comes into play when choosing the correct sized crankbait. Whenever possible match your lure size and color to the food the predator fish are eating. For example, if the walleyes are taking advantage of a heavy hatch of young of the year perch, you will want to match the color and size of the bait to their food preference. Understanding the predator prey relationship in your lake is critical to success.

ADJUSTING FOR DEPTH

Crankbaits are designed to be fished at different depths. This depth determination comes through the size of the lip on the bait. A big lip runs deep and a small lip runs shallow. If the fish you are after are in 15 feet of water, it doesn't do you much good to fish a floating Rapala that dives to five feet. You will not catch those deep fish.

On the flip side, if you are casting a shallow food flat that

When fishing crankbaits it is important to pick the correct style for the situation you are fishing. Crankbaits come in enough variety that you can find one that is the correct size and shape for the species you are after as well as one that will get to the depth you wish to fish.

tops off at 10 feet, it does little good to cast a deep diver that is going to plow a furrow in the bottom on each retrieve. **You need to blend your desired depth with a lure that will get you there.**

There are certain things that you can do to help control the depth of the lure you are using. One is to let out more or less line. More line will get you deeper to a point. Too much line will actually create a bow in your line and bring your lure shallower.

Line diameter is a big factor in determining how deep your lure will run. Heavy line will cause more resistance in the water and will keep your lure shallower. Many anglers are finding the "super lines," like Spiderwire and Fireline, will give you the strength needed but have a smaller diameter to help you get deeper without adding weight. If you do a lot of crankbait trolling, give these "super lines" a try.

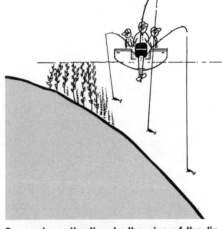

By paying attention to the size of the lip, the shape of the body and diameter of your line, you can easily get crankbaits to run at different depths. Trolling at different depths allows you to effectively cover drop-off areas.

COLOR

I wish I had a nickel for every time someone has asked me about my favorite colors to use for fishing, especially crankbaits. The color I like to use most is the one that is catching fish. That can change from day to day. However, I do have some favorite "go to" colors that I try before others.

One color I have had great success with is firetiger. This is frequently my first choice in color selection. If firetiger isn't doing it I will usually go to a blue and silver. I believe blue is one of the most underutilized colors we have.

There are other factors I will consider when picking color. One of those factors is forage base. If the walleyes are gorging themselves on perch, you can be sure that perch is the first color I will tie on. Water clarity is another important factor. If the water is really clear, a neutral color like shad or crawdad can be productive. (I have seen days when this theory runs the exact opposite with the brightest colors working best.) If the water is stained, I might try brighter colors first.

The most important rule of all when choosing color is to use one you have confidence in. Once your "go to" color does not work, then start experimenting. It is also important to remember that fish get conditioned to a color. **If they stop biting on the one you are using, switch colors before you give up on them. A new color may start the bite all over again.**

THE ADVANTAGE OF RATTLES

Of all the senses that fish use for locating and devouring prey, sight is clearly the most important. Biologists have demonstrated in tests that some fish, like bass, are capable of eating in total darkness. They have also proven that fish that grow up in clear water environments rely on sight more heavily than fish that live in water with poor clarity. Fish in water with poor visibility depend more on their other senses for locating fish. In short, fish in murky environments have more highly developed senses than fish in clear water systems.

Anglers can put this knowledge to use. It only stands to reason that adjustments need to be made to your fishing style if you are fishing areas of low visibility. Crankbaits are made to order for this type of environment, especially ones with rattles.

Rattles send out a whole new set of information to fish. It is true that forage fish don't rattle as they move around, but it is also true that rattles will peak the curiosity of predators. Remember, fish are not very smart. What the rattle is telling them is that there is something over there that they can't see. They can feel it swimming and they can hear it so they come to investigate. Once they investigate, visual contact is made and..... well, who knows, maybe you will catch that fish.

Rattles create that little extra edge in some fishing situations. They are probably at their best in water that has poor clarity, but this does not mean they don't add something to your crankbaits anytime they are used.

BETTER THAN LIVE BAIT?

I like to fish live bait because it works well for me. However, there are times when crankbaits are a better option. One of these times is when you have scattered, feeding fish. **Fish that are aggressive will not hesitate to hit artificials. Fish in a negative mood are usually less interested in artificials.**

Many times when the walleyes were just not hitting live bait, I have switched to crankbaits and have done very well. On one particular trip with my wife, we fished live bait rigs for a couple of hours without a good hit. During this time we saw several instances where minnows would squirt out of the water because something was chasing them.

Eventually we switched over to Shad Raps so we could cover more water as well as try to find out what type of fish were harassing the minnows. We only went about 20 yards before Colette caught the first walleye. During the next hour we caught two more walleyes plus several northerns and bass. It was clear that fish wanted something different than slow moving live bait.

SUMMARY

It is difficult to know just when is the right time for crankbaits. As a general rule, you can always catch something on them, even at times when nothing else is working. I believe one reason for this is the speed with which they are moving. Predators don't have a lot of time to think about whether or not they want this lure. If it comes by quickly they just plain strike in an instinctive reaction versus a planned attack.

Speed is an important consideration when using crankbaits. If you are getting follows and some hits but few aggressive strikes, try speeding up the retrieve. In some situations the only way I have been able to catch fish is by cranking as fast as I possibly can or by speed trolling. If crankbaits aren't working, speed up before going slower.

Never fishing crankbaits is the worst thing you can do. They do work and they do catch many species of fish. Investing the time to learn how to use them is a wise fishing decision.

CHAPTER 17: SPINNERBAITS

If there is one fishing lure you do not want to be without, it is the spinnerbait. In the introduction of this book I quoted guide, Dick Winter, with his "there are no rules in fishing" philosophy. I have a great deal of respect for Dick as an angler so when he tells me spinnerbaits are one of his favorite fishing tools, I know I am on the right track by believing in them so strongly.

What makes a spinnerbait so great? I am not exactly sure. It certainly doesn't look like anything that fish would normally eat. At least if there are critters like that in the water, I have never seen them. What I do know is fish, mainly bass and northerns, will smack a spinnerbait when they will touch nothing else.

BASIC INFORMATION

Spinnerbaits are not designed to be used for all fishing situations, but they are adaptable to many. Most spinnerbait fishing is done in shallow water of ten feet or less. Due to the size of the blades used with spinnerbaits and the 'lift' created by the blades spinnerbaits do not fish deep easily.

Spinnerbaits are usually described as single spins with one blade or tandem spins with two blades. Most single spins will have a round Colorado style blade where most tandem spins will have one Colorado and one willow leaf blade.

Each spinnerbait style has different uses. A single spin Colorado will drop faster and fish deeper than a tandem spin. The round style blade will turn faster and give out more "thumping" vibrations for the fish to pick up on. These vibrations are, without a doubt, part of the fish catching ability of the spinnerbait.

Spinnerbaits come in a variety of colors and blade styles. Tandems tend to run shallower than single spins. Pork or plastic trailers can be added to give your bait a bit more action.

On the flip side, willow leaf blades turn slower and give off different flash and vibrations than Colorado blades. The size of the blade makes it more difficult to fish willow leaf tandems as fast or as deep as other styles. The big blade simply creates too much lift when retrieved.

Which is best? Much of that is a matter of personal preference. I know some anglers that fish nothing but tandem blades with willow leafs and others that fish nothing but Colorado blades and single spins. They both catch fish.

As a general rule, if you are fishing deeper water and need a faster drop and quicker retrieve, go with the single spin. If you are fishing shallow water or want a slower, flashier retrieve use the willow leaf or willow leaf tandem.

When choosing colors don't feel like you have to have one of everything on the rack. What you should have is baits that would fall into the light, medium, and dark color patterns. This mean white for light, black, purple, or brown for dark, and yellow or chartreuse for medium. Some anglers really get hung up on blade colors. I do not. If you have a variety of silver, copper, and brass you will do fine. I have also had good luck with blades that are painted.

Often times I will put some type of trailer on my spinnerbait. I have found plastic worms and plastic grubs to work well. I have also had very good luck with pork strips. Both pork and plastic trailers add a little extra wiggle and appeal.

Spinnerbaits are a simple, yet versatile lure that catch fish. They are designed to be fished shallow but can be fished deep by adding extra weight. Spinnerbaits are also extremely weedless. Pictured here is Todd Amenrud with a bass that couldn't resist the spinnerbait temptation.

MANY USES

Spinnerbaits are an extremely versatile lure. For instance, they are incredibly weedless. They can be used in lily pads, rushes, cabbage, coontail, and many other weeds. The shape of the wire bend acts as a weed guard and keeps the hook quite weed free. The only exception to this is when you are fishing soft weeds. Soft weeds will pull loose and wrap around the blade and cause your lure to foul. Spinnerbaits do not work well in soft weeds.

As a search bait, spinnerbaits cannot be beat. They can be fan casted and retrieved as you work shallow food flats. This ability to keep moving allows you to cover a great deal of water in a hurry and pick up the scattered, active fish. If a heavy concentration is found, I would probably switch over to a more precise bait such as a jig or plastic worm.

Many anglers use nothing but a straight retrieve. I feel that there are more options. One variation that can be used with a spinnerbait is to buzz it across the surface. This is more easily done with single spin Colorado blades than with tandem spins or willow leaf blades. To do this you have to start reeling about the time your bait hits the water. This will keep it up high and on the surface. Holding your rod tip up will also help keep the spinner on top of the water.

Fish are real suckers for falling baits. By using a stop and go retrieve or a jigging retrieve you can often trigger strikes that you couldn't get with a straight retrieve. If you can visually see pockets and weed edges be sure to stop your retrieve and let your spinner helicopter into the depths. This slow falling lure is very tempting. **There is no one set retrieve for spinnerbaits. Each day is different so be sure to experiment.**

Casting is not the only method of fishing spinnerbaits. I see lots of anglers trolling them. Trolling certainly works and will allow you to cover a lot of water in a hurry. Trolling does limit your ability to work different depths and limits your retrieve options, but it also does catch fish so don't be afraid to try it.

DEEP WATER TROLLING

Spinnerbaits also work well for trolling deep water for northerns. Although I rarely see other anglers using this presentation, it can be a fish killer. By adding extra weight above your spinnerbait you can get this lure to the deep weedline and below. I like to put a sucker minnow on this rig for a little extra attraction and smell. It doesn't matter if your minnow is alive or dead, northerns will hit it just the same.

SUMMARY

If you are after northerns or bass, spinnerbaits are truly a great fishing lure. In reality they are little more than an extension of a jig. Like the jig, they are easy to fish, extremely versatile and are proven fish catching tools. They can be buzzed across the surface, fished in shallow weeds, or in deep water. They can be used with live bait or trailers. Spinnerbaits just plain catch fish!

CHAPTER 18:
PLASTIC WORMS

I am always amazed at how few anglers fish a plastic worm. When I ask about them at seminars, I rarely have more than a few people that use them on a regular basis. Maybe this is because they look a little too simple. Maybe it is because some anglers don't like to catch bass. Maybe it is because of a dozen other reasons. **Whatever the reason, if you like to catch fish and are not fishing plastic worms, you are making a huge angling mistake.**

In my opinion, plastic worms are the most underutilized artificial bait on the market. They are an absolute fish killer for many species of fish. Yes, it is true that they are designed to be more of a bass lure, but they catch far more than bass. And when it comes to bass, there is nothing that is better in all around versatility or productivity.

Plastic worms are one of the most underutilized artificial baits we have. They just plain catch fish! If you are not fishing plastic worms, you are making a huge fishing mistake!

THE JIGWORM

Of all the ways of fishing a plastic worm, my favorite is what I call the "jigworm." The jigworm is just another example of how versatile the jig itself is. The jigworm works well for me in places that have tough weeds. I do not use it when the weeds are soft or too thick. Cabbage is great for jigworm fishing.

With a jigworm, you are fishing an exposed hook. Because of this exposed hook it is not totally weedless and can't be fished

I have found that a plastic worm and jighead, or jigworm as I like to call it, is actually my go to bass rig. Although not as weedless as the Texas rig, I find that I can usually catch more fish on this outfit than on Texas rigs. My favorite combination is a 1/8 ounce jighead and a four inch Culprit worm.

in all situations. I like the exposed hook for two reasons. First, I feel I have a better hooking percentage over a weedless rig. With the exposed hook I can bury the barb into the tough mouth easier. Second, the exposed hook occasionally hangs up on weeds.

It may sound funny to hear an angler say that he likes getting stuck in the weeds, but actually, there are times when it can be helpful. If I am fishing cabbage and my jig gets stuck on a leaf visualize what the fish are seeing. They are seeing something that was swimming and is now resting on a weed. They are watching the lure closely as I shake it and then rip it loose. When the jig rips loose and darts away, bass will hit.

My all time favorite jigworm combination is a 1/8 ounce jighead and a four inch Culprit worm. For some reason this four inch worm catches more fish than larger ones. Once I am on a school of fish, I may switch to longer worms or a pig and jig. I have also found that with four inch worms I catch a wider variety of fish including crappies, northerns, and walleyes.

THE TEXAS RIG

Probably the most popular method of fishing a plastic worm is the Texas Rig. This is a very weedless presentation that can be fished anywhere. It goes through lily pads, rushes, cattails, or anything else you can find that bass will hide in.

When talking with anglers that have never fished a Texas worm, I tell them to fish it in the back yard

Although designed to be a bass lure, plastic worms really do catch a variety of fish such as this walleye held by my brother, Jeff. During a day of worm fishing it is not uncommon to catch bass, northerns, crappies, sunnies, and walleyes.

first. By watching your lure in the grass you can get a good idea of the hops and twitches that are necessary to make this worm look real and appetizing. You can also experiment with it in shallow water where you can watch it work.

Bass don't hit this rig hard. As a general rule you will feel a slight 'tick' when a pick up takes place. When a strike does occur you need to be ready to reel up the slack and set the hook hard! When fishing a Texas worm I always set the hook a second time just to make sure.

Many anglers that I know tend to fish plastic worms too fast. It is a very slow presentation and is not meant to be a good search bait. When this bait is fished too fast it does not stay on the bottom as it should. Fishing it slow keeps it on the bottom all the way back to the boat.

No matter what type of plastic worm you are fishing, you will find that many strikes occur as the worm is making its initial drop. This means you **Texas rigged worms are weedless and easy to fish. The most important aspect of fishing them is to go slow and stay on the bottom. Pick-ups are sometimes quite subtle so when in doubt, set the hook!**

always need to be watching your line when you cast. You will be able to see your line jump when a fish hits. Sometimes you will also see it start moving off to the side indicating a fish is swimming with it.

SCENT

There is a lot of controversy about the importance of scent in plastic worms. I have used a variety of scented worms including Mann's flavored worms and Berkley's Power Worms. I have caught fish on both. In my opinion, scent of different types does help. There have been several instances when I have burned a school of bass to the point that I can't get any more to bite. By putting a heavy dose of Dr. Juice or Berkley Strike on the worm, I can usually get one or two more bass out of that school.

Recently, I have started to use a Culprit product called the Burst Worm. This worm actually has a hollow chamber that you fill with a scent and taste stimulant. When fish strike this worm

Scent makes plastic worms even more appealing. Culprit has introduced a new line of worms that have a chamber you fill with scent and taste stimulant. When the fish hits, its mouth is filled with a "burst" of taste. Hence the name Burst Worm.

the gel in the hollow chamber oozes out into their mouths and they get a "burst" of real food taste. They don't let go very easy once they think they have the real thing.

TEXTURE

I believe that texture is very important when choosing your plastic worms. I want a worm that is going to be very soft and supple so that it moves with the slightest twitch and feels like food when the bass inhales it. Texture and scent are two aspects of worm fishing that need careful consideration.

SUMMARY

You probably have been able to tell that I am pretty high on fishing plastic worms. There is a reason for this. I like to catch fish. There have been many days when the only action I got was on plastic worms. It is true that I like to fish walleyes, but if walleyes are not biting, or the lake I am on does not have a good walleye population, I am going to fish for bass.

Plastic worms are not difficult to fish. My daughter, Shelley and her husband, Anders Berg, caught these bass the first time they ever fished plastic worms.

The plastic worm is a deadly bait because it is able to root fish out of the weeds so effectively. It is a simple looking bait that doesn't appear to have much appeal. This may be part of the reason that more people don't fish it.

If you are not interested in fishing plastic worms, at least buy some to put on your jigs or spinnerbaits. This extra attraction added onto your other lures will help convince you of the power of the worm.

CHAPTER 19:
WEATHER AND COLD FRONTS

It is impossible to talk about fish location without discussing weather. Weather is such a huge factor in fish location and fish activity that I don't think we even have a clue as to the magnitude of power weather has over fish behavior. This is not just true of fish, this is true of other animals as well. Ask hunters how weather impacts animal movement and overall success. They will tell you the same thing an angler will tell you. Weather greatly influences animal activity.

There are very few days that I let weather dictate my decision to go fishing. Heavy rain will keep me home as will lightning. Other than that, I will go fishing if my schedule allows it. However, when it comes to planning my fishing outings, if I have choices there are certain times that I like to head for the lake and certain conditions that I try to avoid if possible.

Of all the times to go fishing, I feel that stable weather is definitely the best. If I could order weather for fishing I would order medium south to west winds, partly cloudy, and the fourth or fifth day of a moderately humid warm front. I find a day like this is not only okay for fishing it is great for comfort. Another fish catching ingredient, a falling barometer wouldn't hurt either.

We all know that putting together five days of mild, stable weather is a real rarity in the Midwest. It just does not happen. Instead, our summer weather patterns have us on a jet stream that will bring in front after front after front. Lots of times we have more than one front go through in a day!

When I refer to a front, I am sure that most of you think of a cold front. This isn't necessarily so. Any weather system that brings in a change of conditions is considered a front. I even consider a small ripple in the atmosphere that roars through creating a wind change or a storm a front.

COLD FRONTS

Most of us associate cold fronts with terrible fishing, and for good reason. It generally is terrible fishing! Cold fronts pretty much destroy a good bite. There are, however, different stages of a cold front that make for different fish activity.

I once did some guiding on a lake near Hayward Wisconsin called Namakagan. The day we arrived to do some prefishing was beautiful. It was quite hot with temps near 90, sunny, and humid. The fish were active and life was good. And then it came, the cold front of all cold fronts. The temperature dropped 50 degrees that night. We had rain, wind, fog, more rain and lots more wind. Needless to say, the fishing changed as abruptly and drastically as the weather.

The next day we had to meet with the anglers that we were to take fishing and give them the bad news. They weren't thrilled. However, I will never forget the comment made by one thoughtful angler. He wanted to know how the fishing would be after the weather cleared, the skies turned crystal clear, and the wind switched to the northwest. This was a good point.

At times when fishing is tough you have to be willing to take what you can get. This may mean switching fish species. Pictured are Gary Iskierka and Mike Howard with a mess of cold front crappies.

For the next two days we fished in cold, wet, windy conditions. Fishing was tough but we did catch fish. It was when the sky cleared that the fishing really got tough. The fish that had been turned off before were now impossible to find. I would have very willingly returned to the weather of the previous two days instead of facing the clear conditions.

We left before the fish ever turned on again. I have not been back since.

Cold fronts do not have to be of this magnitude to totally disrupt the underwater world. Cold fronts of lesser intensity can have the same effect. This has been driven home to me time and time again.

One of the more recent memories that comes to mind happened on an early summer guide trip. The week prior to the guide trip had been quite stable with warm temperatures and south winds. On this particular day the forecast was for more of the same with a chance of late afternoon showers. As it turned out the showers were developing as we arrived at the lake.

We did manage a half hour on the water before common sense took over and we headed for the landing. During this first half hour we boated only one fish, a 21 inch walleye. The impressive detail that I remember most was the quantity of fish that were showing up on the locator screen. The deep weedline on down was filled with baitfish and other larger hooks.

Our stay on shore was uneventful. The rain passed east of us and all we received was the wind. Forty minutes later we were back on the same spot that the walleye had come from. The problem was the fish were gone. The pre-front activity that we had observed was now over. I did not have another bite the rest of the day.

SURVIVING A FRONT

Fronts do affect fishing but what can we do about it? Some days, nothing. Some days fishing is going to be impossible and that is that. As a general rule, however, post-front fishing is salvageable with a little modification in your presentation.

Fronts take the aggressiveness out of fish. They shrink the strike zone. Fish are less apt to chase bait and more apt to watch it swim by. In order to be successful in post-frontal conditions you need to make an offer to fish they can't refuse. This can be done in several different ways.

One alternative is to use the best live bait you can get your hands on. You want this live bait to be the wiggliest, squirmiest, stuff you can locate. You may also find that smaller is better than larger. More than likely you will need to fish this lively bait slower and possibly at a different depth.

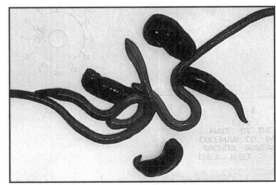

When fishing is tough because of weather changes you need to give yourself every edge you can. One consideration is to use the very best live bait you can find.

Depth can be quite crucial during a front. I have found one of two things to happen. Either the fish go deeper or they go tighter to the weeds. This will depend on the lake as well as the species of fish. Walleyes will tend to go deeper. Bass will often bury into thicker weeds, and northerns may do either. Panfish will usually do both meaning go deeper and into the weeds.

If you have been getting fish on the deep weedline you will need to fish the weedline as tight as you possibly can. Remember, **fish have a small strike zone in frontal conditions and you need to get the bait right in front of their noses before they will accept the offering.**

Walleyes and northerns will often go deeper. How deep is hard to say. Most of the time it will be five to ten feet but for walleyes it could be 20 feet. You will have to depend on your electronics to help you.

FISH SLOWER

Fishing slower can be critical during tough times. Although this can mean simply slowing down on your troll there are other means of fishing slower. One of the better anglers that I know, Randy Amenrud, tends to slow down his presentation by fishing a light jig tipped with live bait. Amenrud will tell you that a light jig will fall

Cold front fishing often means being happy with fewer and smaller fish. This cold front walleye, caught by Kurt Amundson, fell victim to a Foxee Jig and fathead minnow.

slower and stay in front of a stubborn fish longer. I have also seen him change his presentation from a jigging retrieve to a slow swim.

Something else that Amenrud strongly recommends is to keep moving. **You will not find a school of active fish after a front. What you will find is a fish or two out of a school that will be willing to bite.** Once those fish are caught and nothing else is happening, you will need to keep looking for more active biters in a different location.

One additional method of slowing your presentation down is with slip bobbers. Slip bobbers may not provide fast and furious action, but they may provide some action. Some action is better than no action.

LIGHT LINE

One other little tidbit that may help in luring finicky fish into biting is light line. Many times I have witnessed situations where the only bites you get will come on super light line. For walleyes this means four-pound-test and for panfish, two-pound-test.

SUMMARY

Fronts are never fun to fish but they don't have to end your fishing. By slowing down, using live bait, fishing deeper, in the weeds, moving often, and by fishing with the lightest possible line you can get by with, you can be successful.

CHAPTER 20: THE RIGHT LINE

THE PROPERTIES OF MONOFILAMENT

There is an old saying that to lose a good fish through broken line you have to have two jerks...one on each end of the line. Unfortunately there is some truth to this statement. Many fish are lost because the angler did not play the fish properly. The most critical time for playing your fish is when it is close to the boat or to shore.

Monofilament line has a lot of stretch with 25% to 30% quite common. If you have ever been snagged and tried to break your line you have had a chance to experience the stretch in mono. This stretch factor works both for you and against you when fishing.

Your line is the only thing that connects you to the fish. The extra dollars you spend to buy quality brands is well worth the money.

STRETCH

When you are setting the hook on a fish you are combating the effects of stretch. Fish have bony, tough mouths that can be hard to penetrate with a hook. Combine this with line stretch and you have the ingredients for a fish that is hard to hook. This is the reason that many young or novice anglers lose fish right after the strike. They never deliver the power necessary to drive the hook home.

To better understand the effects of stretch when setting the hook, try this easy experiment. Take your favorite fishing rod out into the backyard, remove the hooks and peel out about 30 yards of line. Now have your fishing buddy set the hook while you hang onto the other end. You will be amazed at how little pressure is generated by the hook set. This activity will help you understand the effects of line stretch and help you realize that in many situations, setting the hook more than once is recommended.

Once a fish is hooked, line stretch can work in your favor. When fish make a power run it is difficult to keep up with them by manipulation of the rod and reel. Line stretch will actually help you play the fish and put some "forgiveness" into the fight. How-ever, after the fish is close to the boat, there is no longer enough line out to allow the stretch factor to really help you in fighting the fish. When a fish makes a power run close to the boat, the line takes a lot more pressure and will break. This is why most fish are lost close to the boat.

SETTING YOUR DRAG

The drag on your reel is designed to help anglers fight a fish. Drags are supposed to "slip" so that the line does not break. All too often this is not the case. Drags are usually set too tight. **To really set your drag properly you need to have someone hang onto the line where it comes off the end of the pole. This is the best place to check your drag because this is where the fish is checking the drag.**

Most anglers that I know set the drag by pulling the line where it comes out of the reel. Although this gives you some indication of the drag setting, pressure here is much different than pressure on your line when the rod is bent. Learning to set your drag properly will help you land that quality fish when it does strike.

The proper way to set your drag is to pull on your line where the fish pulls on it, not at the reel.

Many times I see anglers set their drags quite light just to be on the safe side. This can be a disaster! A light drag means that your reel will slip easily. **If you turn the crank when the drag is slipping you are putting twist in your line.** A four-to-one pick up on your reel means that every time you turn your reel handle once with no line coming in, you have put four twists in your line. Twisted line is a recipe for a short fishing trip.

Young and beginning anglers have an especially hard time with this concept. Because of this it is extremely important to teach anglers to pump a fish. Pumping prevents line twist and is something that can be practiced in the backyard before going to the lake.

BACKREELING

Learning how to backreel is a skill that anglers need to know. Backreeling means you turn off your anti-reverse so that your reel turns either way. When a fish is putting heavy pressure on your line you "backreel" to feed out line instead of relying on your drag.

Learn to switch your anti reverse button off when fighting a fish. This will allow you to backreel when the fish applies pressure and will reduce your dependency on your drag.

This allows you to set your drag a bit tighter and still play a fish safely. Backreeling is especially effective when fish are close to the boat.

One other positive aspect of backreeling has to do with line twist. I have found that because you can set your drag tighter when backreeling, you have less tendency to "reel" when the drag is slipping.

Backreeling is not just for those times when you have a big fish on. If I am fishing crappies with two-pound-test line I will definitely backreel if the fish is fighting tough. If I am using four-pound-test leaders for walleyes I may have to backreel on every fish. **Backreeling simply gives you more control over the fish and lets you fight the fish according to the equipment and line weight you are using.**

REMOVING THE TWIST

No matter how careful you are when fishing, you will eventually run into a situation where you have twisted line. Twisted line does not mean that you have to throw it all away and start over. It usually means you just need to eliminate the twist. This can be easily done.

If you own a boat follow this procedure. First, cut everything off of your line including your snap swivel if you have one. Next, start trolling the line out behind the boat just like you were fishing. The friction of the water will pull the line out once you have it started. Let out as much line as you feel is twisted and reel it back in. The tension of the water will pull all of the twist out of your line and it will reel in perfectly straight.

If you do not have a boat, there is another option. Again, untie everything from your line, set your rod down in the grass and walk your line across the yard. Once you have 30-40 yards out, simply lay your line in the grass, walk back to your rod and reel it in. The friction of the grass will help reduce the twists. You may have to do this a couple of times to get all of the twists out of your mono.

CHOOSING THE CORRECT WEIGHT LINE

Over the years, I have had many people ask me what kind of line is best and what weight line they should use. As for the brand, much of that is a matter of personal preference. I recommend using a quality monofilament. Personally, I have found Stren Easy Cast to be a quality all around monofilament. As far as the correct pound test, that is another matter.

When choosing a pound test for your fishing **you need to choose the lightest line that you can get by with for the conditions you are fishing.** That might be 20-pound-test or it might be two-pound-test. Again, it depends on the conditions you are fishing.

LIGHT LINE CATCHES MORE FISH

I have seen proof too many times to dispute the fact that light line catches more fish. There are days, most days, when it probably does not make a bit of difference, but then there are times when it makes **all** of the difference.

One spring I was fishing crappies in a back bay of a small lake. The crappies were spending their time in a small depression in this bay. This fact was no secret. We were one of four boats casting to this spot. At the end of the evening one boat left with three fish, one left with one fish, one left with zero fish, and we left with 13. The only difference between what we were doing and they were doing was the fact that we were using two-pound-test Stren Magnathin.

Usually I don't use such light line for crappies. Usually four-pound-test works fine. However, on this particular night, the fish were in a very negative mood and it took the light line to make a difference.

I have experienced this same scenario with walleyes. There have been times when using four-pound-test leaders was the only

When conditions are tough you will find that light line will catch more fish. On this particular day two-pound-test line was needed to tempt the finicky crappies.

way that you could get a bite. Again, this is not the norm but it does happen. You need to be prepared for this type of fishing situation.

Many anglers feel you can't catch big fish on such light line. That is not true. If you fight the fish properly and back-reel, you can take a very large fish on light line. The biggest walleye and northern I have ever caught have both come on ultra light rigs.

THE DIFFERENCE IN TEETH

I have seen anglers use steel leaders for walleye fishing because they are afraid that the sharp teeth of the walleye will cut their line. This is not true. Walleyes do have sharp teeth but their teeth are shaped like round toothpicks and are sharp only at the tips. **Walleye teeth do not cut line.**

And then there are northerns. Northerns have teeth that are shaped like daggers. Their teeth are sharp on the sides as well as at the tip. Northerns can cut very heavy line with their teeth causing anglers to resort to the use of steel leaders.

Even though northerns have teeth that will readily cut line, many anglers prefer **not** to use steel leaders when fishing for northerns. They understand they may lose a few fish but also understand that **the more garbage you hang on your line, the fewer strikes you will have.** If you are fishing for large northerns and do need a steel leader, **use the shortest one you can get by with.** I prefer to use one that is black as well. I do not like the extra shine created by a silver leader.

CHAPTER 21: EXPECTATIONS AND MEMORIES

I started this book by explaining that fishing is a sport you can never hope to master. I am ending this book with the same premise. No matter how much you know about fishing, you can never learn it all. You can never hope to become an expert that can catch fish of any size and any species on any lake at will. It just isn't that way.

What you do learn about fishing is that you can improve your skills. You can start catching more fish on a more consistent basis, but it takes time. You have to work at it.

One method of becoming a better angler is to read material such as this book. **This book is my own personal perspective of what works well for me. There are certainly other methods and techniques that have not been addressed in this book.** That is how it should be. By reading and learning from other anglers you will gain information that can be blended with what you already know and blended with the methods and styles of fishing you prefer.

Do not stop thinking. When it comes right down to it there really are no rules for catching fish other than you have to find them first. **You need to continually puzzle out what is happening on a lake each day you are fishing.** Every day is a different day. There are no guarantees. Because fish are not where you expect them to be or because they are not where they were

You don't have to travel to the ends of the earth to have good fishing. Many times it is a matter of understanding where to look for fish and to use some common sense.

yesterday, does not mean your outing is a disaster. You need to keep looking for fish. Fish are constantly changing their location on water systems. These changes are due to baitfish, weeds, water temperature, seasons, and a host of other reasons.

Do not get into the rut of fishing memories. This is a very dangerous pattern because it eliminates thinking and invites failure. By going to a lake with a plan of attack, you will program second and third and fourth options into your day. This keeps the mind working and defeat at bay. Randy Amenrud's fishing philosophy is that you "never get skunked when you go fishing, you just run out of time." There is some truth to this. If you go home empty it simply means that you have not had enough time to figure out the pattern for that particular day.

Learn how to be a multiple species angler. By learning how to fish for many species of fish in different situations, you gain extensive knowledge that can be used over and over. **'One species anglers' are one dimensional and have limited their ability to catch any species of fish, including the one they are after.**

APPEAL TO THE SENSES

The only way that you can ever catch a fish is to fool it into thinking that your bait or lure is something good to eat. The only way you can catch a fish is to convince it that your offering should go to its stomach.

Fish don't have hands to test items in their environment. They do this with their mouths. Their mouths are the testing laboratories they use to determine if something is good to eat. If they don't like it they simply spit it out. This is done quickly. Fish can inhale your bait, taste it, feels its texture, and spit it out in less than half a second. This is much too fast for our human reflexes.

In order for us to catch a fish we have to have that fish keep the bait in its mouth long enough for us to detect the bite and set the hook. Many times we are too slow with the hook setting process.

To catch fish you need to appeal to their senses. The more senses you can appeal to, the greater chance you have of being successful. Sometimes live bait is the key. Often times live bait, used in conjunction with artificials, is even better. **Adapt your fishing approach to appeal to as many senses as you can for the particular fishing situation you are experiencing.**

ONE LAST THOUGHT

If you enjoy the sport of fishing, please take the time to pass it on to others. In our busy and hectic world, fewer and fewer people have the opportunity to experience fishing. Fishing is not only a wonderful pastime, it helps us connect with nature and understand the complexity of the world we live in. The kids of today will have to take care of the world and environment tomorrow. **We cannot expect them to take care of a world they do not understand.**

Fishing is one way that kids can see the beauty of nature as well as understand the cruelty of the 'eat and be eaten' world we live in. Fishing brings us into nature and brings nature to us. Fishing is one way to help ensure that our world will be taken care of in the future long after we are gone.

Good luck fishing.

Fishing is a great sport that can be enjoyed for a lifetime. Family fishing memories, such as this, are remembered and cherished forever.